The Telephone Murder

The Mysterious Death of Julia Wallace

William and Julia Wallace

The Telephone Murder

The Mysterious Death of Julia Wallace

by
Ronald Bartle

WS
&H

Wildy, Simmonds & Hill Publishing

The Telephone Murder: The Mysterious Death of Julia Wallace

British Library Cataloguing in Publication Data
A catalogue record for this book is available from the British Library

ISBN 9780854901029

Printed and bound in the United Kingdom by Antony Rowe Ltd, Chippen-
ham, Wiltshire

First published in 2012 by
Wildy, Simmonds & Hill Publishing
58 Carey Street
London WC2A 2JF
England

To my wife Molly
with grateful thanks for all
her enthusiastic encouragement

CONTENTS

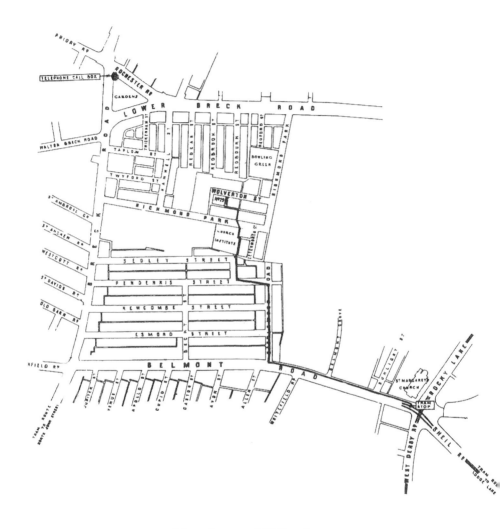

Map of area and Wallace's route

INTRODUCTION TO THE WALLACE CASE 1931

The case of William Herbert Wallace is unique in the annals of English criminal law. It has been so regarded by lawyers, authors and criminologists since 1931 when it took place. Not so publicly known as the cases of Crippin, Palmer, Heath or Haigh, nor featuring so dramatic a serial killer as the ever illusive Jack the Ripper, it presents a baffling mystery which far exceeds any of these other causes célèbres. For here was a mild mannered and apparently inoffensive insurance agent charged with the savagely brutal murder of his wife, with whom according to those who knew them well, he lived on terms of marital peace and contentment and had done so for many years. It seemed incredible that such a man, after so many years of harmonious marriage, should batter his wife to death in what was described at his trial as a 'frenzied attack'. Moreover, the nature of the crime appeared inconsistent with the case presented against Wallace by the prosecution in the trial.

The Crown presented the case to the jury as a carefully and coldly planned killing, almost an assassination. This, it was argued, was no run-of-the mill husband and wife murder, no unforeseen consequence of a dispute which had got out of hand when the firm balance of controlled emotion had spilt over into blind fury. By common consent of those on both sides of the court the whole act was meticulously planned and ruthlessly carried out. Yet, notwithstanding the shocking nature of the deed, guilt was never finally established.

Criminologists and writers, jurists and forensic experts, some of whom have spent years studying the case, have been unable to agree as to the guilt or innocence of William Herbert Wallace. Prominent authors of books on the subject show that differences of opinion remain. W F Wyndham-Brown in his book, *The Trial of William Herbert Wallace* (Gollancz, 1933), endorses a general judicial view that there is a just cause for grave suspicion about Wallace, but no direct evidence on which a verdict of guilty could be justified. However in what has been considered the standard work on the topic *The Killing of Julia Wallace* (Charles Scibner's Sons, 1969), Jonathan Goodman is emphatically in favour of the innocence of Wallace and points the accusing finger at another party. A similar standpoint is taken by Roger Wilkes in *Wallace, the Final Verdict* (Bodley Head, 1984)" where he maintains that there is a much stronger case against a former fellow employee of Wallace, Richard Gordon Parry. Nevertheless in *The murder of Julia Wallace* (Bluecoat Press, 2001), James Murphy, who has devoted much research and labour to a close analysis of the Wallace drama, has no doubt that the guilty verdict of the jury was correct and that the weight of the circumstantial evidence should have been decisive for conviction.

It is not surprising that Edward Hemmerde, the chief prosecuting counsel at the trial, his junior and also Detective Superintendent Hubert Moore who led the police investigation were certain of Wallace's guilt, while those in charge of the defence took a different view. The opinion of Mr Justice Wright, the distinguished judge who presided at the hearing at Liverpool Spring Assizes on 22 April 1931, expressed many years later, is interesting:

> Never forget that Wallace was a chess player. I should say that, broadly speaking, any man with common sense would have said that Wallace's alibi was too good to be true, but that is not an argument you can hang a man on. So many strange things happen in life. I should not and never did demand a motive for any crime, very often the motive is merely impulse and you must remember that Wallace was a highly strung man. But if Wallace did murder his wife, as the jury thought, then there might have been a motive… after his trial the station master at Birkenhead station mentioned the case to me as I waited for a train. He said it was the opinion of the people in the district that there was another woman in the case. That certainly never came out at the trial, but at the time I could not help thinking that Wallace found domestic felicity a little boring, as it is apt to be occasionally to anybody.

In any case of a 'domestic murder' that is to say murder of a wife by a husband, or less usually of a husband by a wife, it is well worth taking a careful look at the background of the parties concerned and the environment in which the crime is committed. The house in which Wallace lived, 29 Wolverton Street in Liverpool, was a terraced house in a cheerless cul-de-sac of similar dwellings typical of the drab, lower middle class area in which it stood. Three of the houses had been the scene of suicide and two more of bereavement in tragic circumstances. The others had received the attention of local burglars who had escaped arrest.

William Herbert Wallace was born on the 29 August 1878, the eldest of three children of working class parents. He was an intelligent child at school and it may well be said of him that he was one of those people who should and could have gone further in his later life had his intellectual gifts and his energies been better directed. After leaving school at 14 he became a linen-draper's assistant for six years and then spent three years in

Manchester employed with a wholesale textile factory. However, Wallace sought a more interesting life and in 1902 he sailed to Calcutta where he gained employment as a salesman in a trading company. Three years later he travelled to Shanghai where his younger brother Joseph was working. He became advertising manager in a general store. However, Wallace suffered the curse of ill-health in his career. He was plagued by serious kidney disease and was obliged to return to England where, in 1907, he had his left kidney removed. In due course he moved to Harrogate. There he landed a job as an agent for the Liberal Party and it was there that he met and, in 1914, married his wife Julia.

During the Great War the pair moved to Liverpool. Wallace, who was unfit for military service, was by then working for the Prudential Insurance Company as an agent at a salary of £260 a year. That sum was fully adequate to cover a very modest rent for their home at 29 Wolverton Street. From that time onwards until 20 January 1931, when Julia was murdered, there is little of interest in the life together of Julia and William Wallace. According to Wallace the marriage was blissfully peaceful, although some witnesses have thrown doubt upon that description. The pair could hardly have been called particularly sociable. Their neighbours at 31 Wolverton Street only visited them on three occasions in 16 years.

The Wallaces remained childless but they retained and practised their interests. In the case of William these consisted of chess, the practice of chemical experiments and the study of Stoicism. For her part Julia spoke fluent French and played the piano with considerable skill. Their shared love of music induced Wallace to achieve a fairly rudimentary knowledge of the violin, and together they would play duets, Wallace on the violin and Julia at the piano. Their social life seems to have been fairly limited, consisting of occasional visits by friends, including Wallace's sister-in-law, and more rarely by business associates. It was into this placid environment that there came the terrible events of the 20 January 1931.

The catalyst for murder was, of all things, a telephone call. Wallace was a keen though not very expert chess player. The club which he belonged to, the Central Chess Club, conducted its activities in the City Café in the Anfield district of Liverpool. Wallace, who regularly attended the club for play, arrived at the café at about 7.40pm on Monday 19 January. According to Wallace when subsequently interviewed by the police, he had not informed anyone other than his wife that he would be at the club that night. Soon after his arrival, when he had commenced a game, he was informed by Samuel Beattie, the club captain, that there had been a telephone message for him at about 7.20pm. The caller left the name of R M Qualtrough and said that he wanted to see Wallace at 7.30pm the next day at his address, which he gave as 25 Menlove Gardens East. The caller said that it was 'something in the nature of his, that is Wallace's business'. The Menlove Gardens area was in the district of Mossley Hill. In fact both name and address were fictitious. Wallace displayed puzzlement over both. He said he knew nobody of the name of Qualtrough and that he was not familiar with the Menlove Gardens area, although he had heard of it. He decided to look for the address next day.

On Tuesday 20 January, after completing his normal round as an agent for the Prudential, he set off for Menlove Gardens East. The search proved fruitless; he asked no fewer than nine people the whereabouts of Menlove Gardens East without success. Finally at about 8pm he gave up the search and returned home. He arrived at his address at 8.45pm. His two neighbours from number 31 were just leaving.

After a short conversation with them Wallace attempted to enter his house. They decided to wait to see that all was well. After experiencing some difficulty with both the front door and the back door, Wallace entered the house by the back door and made a quick search of the premises. When he entered the parlour a scene of utter horror met his eyes. The body of Julia Wallace lay face down on the rug in front of the fire. Her head was surrounded by a pool of blood which had seeped into the carpet and splashed onto the walls. Her skull had been crushed by no fewer than 11 blows delivered with great force. The blow that killed her was the one delivered to her left temple; this was the first. The wound was open revealing brain matter and bone. There were signs of a burglary having taken place, but none of breaking and entering. However the sum taken was small, about £4 in cash, a crossed cheque and a postal order. Strangely the thief had closed the lid of the box from which it had been taken and had replaced the box. None of Julia Wallace's jewellery had been taken. In a jar in a bedroom were a few £1 notes one of which was smeared with blood, these had not been removed. Across the shoulders of the corpse was Wallace's mackintosh. This was stained with blood and partially burnt. There were further signs of disturbance in the house which the police believed to be an attempt by the murderer to give the impression that the crime was a theft which went badly wrong.

The premises were thoroughly searched by the police but little came to light to assist in their investigations. The forensic expert who examined the body was Professor John Edward Whitely MacFall. MacFall, instead of performing such basic tests as establishing the temperature of the body and of the parlour, based his deductions solely on the evidence of rigor mortis that had set into the neck and left arm, and on the clotting of the blood that had spilled from Julia's head wounds. This method left room for a wide margin of error as to the time of the assault, which was described by MacFall as 'frenzied'.

The Liverpool police, under the direction of Detective Superintendent Hubert Moore, began their investigations. Writers who favour the view that Wallace was innocent have criticised the police on various grounds. This is not surprising since it complements their theory that Wallace should not have been charged with the crime. However, in the view of this author, the Liverpool police exercised thoroughness and a fair degree of efficiency in their investigation of a case which by any standards was baffling in the extreme.

There were several factors which made the task of the police difficult from the beginning. Firstly, the apparent absence of any motive and the reported tranquillity of the Wallace's marriage made the situation seem very different from the average domestic murder. The trivial sum that was missing and the fact that a further sum of money and jewellery were left untouched made theft as a motive seem unlikely. The mysterious telephone call which provided Wallace with an alibi, and the absence of any alternative suspect whom Julia knew well enough to admit to the house were further considerations. In these circumstances it is not surprising that Wallace himself did not escape suspicion: 'If not Wallace, then who?' was clearly an important question for the police. In his statements, of which there were several, Wallace persistently protested his innocence. There were four factors which he could pray in aid of his innocence. First, the complete absence of motive; secondly, the alibi created by the phone call; thirdly, the fact that there were no traces of blood on his person; and finally, the time schedule, which would have made it difficult if not impossible for him to commit the murder in the time available.

After his first interview, Wallace told two members of the chess club that he had been cleared. But Detective Superintendent Hubert Moore and his colleagues began to form other ideas. They were particularly influenced by the discovery that the telephone call, purported to be from Mr Qualtrough, had been made from a telephone box which was a mere 400 yards from Wallace's house.

When Wallace set off on his search for the fictitious 25 Menlove Gardens East he went to Smithdown Road to catch his tram. Police trials showed that the journey from his home to the tram stop varied between 17 and 20 minutes. He caught the tram at 7.06pm on the evidence of the conductor. The evidence of a milk boy was that he saw Julia Wallace alive at 6.45pm, though he later changed this to about 6.30pm, This schedule would have left very little time for Wallace to carry out the murder and catch the tram by 7.06pm. The second difficulty faced by the police was the absence of any blood on Wallace's clothes. Could he have changed his clothes after Julia Wallace had been killed? (by a method which caused blood to spurt onto the floor and onto the walls)? If so, when and how did he do so? Not withstanding these obstacles Detective Superintendent Moore decided to charge Wallace with the murder. His theory was that Wallace himself had made the call and supplied himself with an alibi. Wallace's reply was: 'what can I say in answer to a charge of which I am absolutely innocent?'

Wallace's trial took place in 22 April 1931 at the Liverpool Spring Assizes. The judge presiding was Mr Justice Wright and the prosecution was conducted by the Recorder of Liverpool Edward George Hemmerde KC. The defendant was represented by Roland Oliver KC. Both leading counsel were very able and experienced advocates. Mr Justice Wright, although experienced in commercial rather than criminal cases, was universally recognised as a brilliant jurist. The jury consisted of 12 persons drawn from an area outside Liverpool itself in order to avoid the danger of prejudice arising from contact with those who lived within the district of the crime.

The case which the prosecution lay before the jury was this: On the evening before the murder, that is Monday 19 January 1931, Wallace left home to attend the chess club in the city café, where he was scheduled to play a match. On his own admission nobody apart from his wife knew that he would be going there on that day or time. On his way to catch a tram he diverted from what would have been his shortest route and visited a telephone call box which was a little, but not greatly, out of his way. It was then that Wallace, in a disguised voice, telephoned the chess club and left a message for himself. Wallace gave his name as R M Qualtrough and he also gave the completely fictitious address of 25 Menlove Gardens East. As Qualtrough he asked that a message be given to Mr Wallace when he arrived at the club that he, Qualtrough, wished Wallace to call at his home the following evening on a matter of business. Counsel then disclosed the fact the telephone box was a mere 400 yards from Wallace's home in Wolverton Street. This was known from the fact that the caller had some difficulty in getting through and, as was the normal practice in this situation, the girl telephonist noted down the time of the call, the number and the location of the call box. As with so many things in the Wallace case, this was an event that could be interpreted both against him and in his favour. On the one hand there was a kiosk which was close to his home and in a quiet spot where he would not be recognised. On the other hand a caller who wanted to cast suspicion on Wallace might deliberately choose the location and then confuse the call to enable it to be traced. When Wallace arrived at the chess club he was informed of the message and pretended complete ignorance of the name and address of the caller. However he said he would look for the address the following evening as requested. The case for the Crown was that Wallace, having provided himself with the requisite alibi, had set the scene for Julia's murder.

On Tuesday 20 January, after his days work as an insurance agent visiting various clients, Wallace set off for 'Menlove Gardens East'. He boarded a tram at 7.06pm having, it was alleged by the Crown, brutally murdered his wife. The defence was that Wallace who had been lured into a wild goose chase by the real murderer, was making a genuine search for the address of the house with which he had been supplied.

Prosecuting counsel made it clear to the jury that the manner of the search pointed to the conclusion that Wallace was setting up a false alibi for himself. During the course of his enquiries Wallace spoke to no fewer than nine people, three of whom told him that there was no such place as Menlove Gardens East. The remainder did not know of it. At no time before setting off on his search did Wallace consult a plan of the area nor telephone his superior in the Prudential who lived at Menlove Gardens West, which could have saved him the journey. On returning to his home Wallace entered his house and after some difficulty with entry found his wife's body on the floor of the parlour, her skull shattered by 11 violent blows. Much was made by the prosecution of the strange lack of emotion on the part of Wallace in the presence of his two neighbours after this discovery. The same was noted by the police and medical expert when they were present in the house.

The hub of the defence centred on two factors in the case. First, the time factor. On the basis of witness statements it was submitted that Wallace did not have the time either to make the telephone call before arriving at the club on the Monday or to murder Mrs Wallace before leaving on his search of Menlove Gardens East. Secondly, the absence of blood on his clothing. Mr Justice Wright in his summing up told the jury that the case against Wallace was based entirely on circumstantial evidence. There is little doubt that the summing up by Mr Justice Wright was for an acquittal. It therefore came as a shock that the jury after only one hours retirement returned a verdict of guilty. Wallace swayed but showed no emotion. He now faced the gallows.

Hector Munro, Wallace's solicitor, lodged notice of appeal. The portents were not good. The Court of Criminal Appeal had never upset the verdict of a jury. The appeal was heard by the Lord Chief Justice Viscount Hewart of Bury with Mr Justice Branson and Mr Justice Hawke. After a long preamble the Lord Chief Justice said 'the conclusion to which we have arrived is that the case against the appellant, which we have carefully and anxiously considered and discussed, was not proven with that certainty which is necessary in order to justify a verdict of guilty'.

Wallace was free, but soon had to move out of the area due to a whispering campaign. He died in February 1933 and was buried next to his wife.

Raymond Chandler was right 'The Wallace case is unbeatable, it will always be unbeatable'. The foregoing is a summary of this extraordinary case. The purpose is to enable the reader to better understand the nature of the events and the person involved. In the subsequent chapters of this work these matters will be dealt with in greater detail; the argument and the aspects both helpful and damaging to Wallace will be carefully weighed and the various views of other writers considered. Finally, this author will provide what he submits is the solution to the mystery, which has puzzled criminal experts for decades, over the case of William Herbert Wallace.

CHAPTER ONE

THE BACKGROUND ENVIRONMENT

Liverpool in 1931 was a great metropolis. Transport was by tram and bus. The area of Wolverton Street, where the Wallace's lived, was lower middle class, grey and characterless. The depression triggered by the Wall Street crash had affected all Europe and in particular the north of England. This was the Anfield area. Most of the property in this part of Liverpool was rented – not owned. In spite of the competitive cheapness of property at that time, most people who occupied the inferior area of a great city could only afford to rent. Anfield was not a slum. The houses were terraced – small but providing a degree of respectable habitation to their occupants. The rents were low enough to make it possible for someone on a modest income to live comfortably. Wallace for example on an annual salary of £260, paid fourteen shillings a week in rent for his house in Wolverton Street. Nevertheless, times were hard for the mass of working class people. Unemployment in the country had reached three million, and there was no welfare state at that time (which has only existed since the Beveridge Report after the Second World War).

A visitor to the poor areas of Liverpool from the more prosperous south of England in 1931 might well have concluded that some things had not greatly improved since the Victorian era. Children still ran bare-foot in the streets, some of which were illuminated by gas lamps. Unemployed men lounged around street corners and wives took in washing as well as lodgers to make ends meet. Foreign competition had dealt a deadly blow to the traditional industry, while the government struggled to cope with mountainous economic and financial problems.

To add to the gloom, the winter of 1930–31 had been bitterly cold, with snow and ice prevalent throughout the city. Such was the environment in January of that year, the month which was the scene of the extraordinary events which follow. But first let us consider the home of the Wallace's, 29 Wolverton Street. Its position and layout form a vital element in the case which has universally been considered as the unsurpassed 'whodunnit?' in the annals of criminal England.

The house in which the Wallace's lived and where the murder of Julia Wallace took place, was a small terraced house typical of the immediate area and identical to the other houses in Wolverton Street. The district in which it was situated was the Richmond Park area of Anfield. Although it was drab and characterless it was far from being a destitute property and the house itself was an improvement on the two-up, two-down accommodation which represented the working-class neighbourhoods. Nevertheless, there would be little about it to attract the buyer of today. The ground floor, typically in keeping with this kind of dwelling, had the usual front room which, again, somewhat in keeping with the cultural standards of the time, was cluttered with various pieces of furniture and other objects which made a fairly small room less comfortable than it might otherwise have been. But the Wallaces, who at the time of the murder had lived in the house for 16 years, found it useful as a 'parlour'. It was here that they entertained their comparatively few visitors.

It was also in this place that they enjoyed musical evenings where Julia played, very competently, the piano and William, less expertly, performed on the violin. It was in this room that the body of the slain Julia Wallace was found. Behind the parlour was the kitchen. This also was completely different from the modern housewife's idea of what a good kitchen should be. On the left hand side of a Victorian oven was a substantial wall bookcase. Some seven feet in height, under which was a cabinet. The adjoining wall supported a desk which provided shelving for a number of books. Under the bookshelves were files and books of accounting, which were used no doubt by Wallace in the course of his work as an insurance agent for the Prudential. A large table occupied the centre of the room around which were scattered chairs of various vintage. This was where William and Julia had their meals and entertained day to day guests. This room fulfilled the purpose of a dining room rather than a kitchen. The kitchen proper was behind the parlour. It contained a gas cooker, a draining board and sink, a kitchen range and such-like objects for the storing and preparation of food. From this room a window looked onto the back yard which contained a coal shed and an outside WC. Access to this back yard was provided by a door from a passage at the rear of the premises.

Upstairs there were three more rooms. The front bedroom was normally not in use, but was available for a visitor who stayed overnight. The centre bedroom was the one used by the Wallace's. It was where Julia Wallace's jewellery and clothes were stored. The room at the back was used by Wallace for chemical experiments, which was a hobby of his. Between the middle and the back room was a bathroom which housed a bath, a wash basin and, behind a partition, a WC. A single staircase connected the ground and the first floors of the premises.

Now let us consider the district in which Wolverton Street was situated. The Anfield area of Liverpool was neither a fashionable nor a working-class district. It was a lower middle class locality with many houses of the same type as the Wallaces. The lay-out of the region immediately surrounding Wolverton Street is of great importance since one of the principal factors in the trial of Wallace for the murder of his wife was the question of the time it would have taken Wallace to walk the distance from his house to a certain telephone box, and also from his house to various tram stops. The main source of transport in Liverpool in 1931 was that of tram cars; buses were far less frequent.

There are two journeys of importance made by Wallace in this case. The first is on 19 January when he left his house and visited the central chess club, and the second on the 20 January when he went to search for the non-existent address of 25 Menlove Gardens East. As to the first, Wallace said that after leaving home he walked along Richmond Park and turned left at the church of the Holy Trinity on the corner. Then he walked down Breck Road, again turned left at the corner with Belmont Road and boarded a tram in Belmont Road for the chess club. This in fact is a longer route to Belmont Road than the more direct one down past the church institute, left into Pendennis Street and down Castlewood Road into Belmont Road. One important issue was why did Wallace, who knew the district very well take the much longer way. Had he turned right instead of left at the church corner this would take him to the junction of Breck Road with Rochester Road.

At this junction stood the telephone kiosk from which the mysterious call by the man called Qualtrough was made. The prosecution case at the trial was that it was in fact Wallace himself who made the phone call and so provided himself with an alibi for the murder of his wife which he then went on to commit. We shall consider these matters at greater length later in this work.

Now let us take a look at the Liverpool City Police; the force which investigated the Wallace case and which decided to arrest and charge him with the murder of his wife. The scientific methods available to police in the investigation of crimes in 1931 were far less developed than they are today. For instance DNA, which can be deduced from blood, saliva or semen for the purpose of identifying a murderer was undiscovered at that time. It was possible to identify blood as belonging to a particular individual but that is all. Consequently, in a case such as this, when there was a dearth of direct evidence as to the guilty party the police were obliged to rely on the less trustworthy, circumstantial evidence to build their case. This could prove to be a desperately difficult task. In a case in which public emotions ran high the police could face fierce criticism from press and public if time passed and the culprit remained at large.

In his book *The Killing of Julia Wallace* Jonathan Goodman is highly critical of the Liverpool police force as it was in 1931. Tracing the inefficiency and alleged corruption in the force to the police strike of 1919, Goodman goes so far as to say 'By 1931 much of the Liverpool city police force was hardly up to the task of dealing with parking offences let alone a full-scale murder investigation'. This would appear to be an extreme judgement.

Even with forensic science on the side of the police, there remain unsolved murder cases. A few, by the application of DNA, are solved some time after they were committed, others remain forever unexplained. In the Wallace case it seems to this author that the police made every effort to get to the bottom of the mystery. They thoroughly examined the premises at Wolverton Street, questioned at length all potential witnesses and suspects, and held frequent conferences during the investigation. Under the efficient direction of Detective Superintendent Hubert Moore it is difficult to see what more the police could have done to get to the bottom of what has always been considered a classic murder mystery.

Since the police based their entire case on the premise that Wallace was the guilty party, it is not surprising that after his final release they closed the book and deduced that they had no further action to take which they felt could have any chance of success. Yet the Liverpool police were not blameless. One serious omission was that detectives made no attempt to find the conductor of the tram which took Wallace to the central chess club on the night of 19 January. This evidence could have proved what time it was that Wallace left Anfield and whether he could have made the telephone call himself. Moreover, the police were clumsy in their search of 29 Wolverton Street. Here it was never clear whether the blood spot on the lavatory bowl or the smear of blood on the pound note in the middle bedroom was caused by the murderer or the police themselves. Thus it was that the police could only supply the prosecution at the trial with a case against Wallace which consisted of purely circumstantial evidence. We shall see how the prosecution made the most of this at the trial.

CHAPTER TWO

THE CHARACTERS OF WILLIAM AND JULIA WALLACE

In any case when murder is suspected of having been committed by a husband two things are of importance. The character of the husband and the prevailing relationship between him and his wife at the time of the murder. There can be a variety of motives for wife murder, some almost pointless.

When Arthur Devereux murdered his wife and her two twins in January 1905 and placed the bodies in a trunk, his only motive was financial desperation over his inability to support his family on a very modest wage. In 1910 Hawley Harvey Crippin was hanged for the murder of his wife Cora. There had been infidelity on both sides contributing to the collapse of the marriage and Cora was taking money out of their joint account. Crippin, like Devereux, was desperate for a new life, but like the former his attempt to escape by murder led him to the gallows. George Smith the 'brides in the bath' killer, callously murdered his three victims between 1912 and 1914, after swindling them out of their money. In June 1920, Harold Greenwood, a solicitor in Wales, was acquitted of the murder of his wife after evidence showed that he could not have the suspected financial motive. In October 1935, Dr Buck Ruxton murdered his common-law wife in a fit of rage.

In murder of one spouse by another, usually a wife by her husband, but much more occasionally the other way round, the motive varies greatly. Usually there has been a breakdown in the relationship which builds to an intolerable situation in which something has to give. Violence in marriage has been reflected in recent times by the 'battered wife's syndrome' but usually the violence is not of a lethal type. Sometimes the catalyst for murder is something more mundane such as a difference over money or a much more trivial cause of complaint. In a case in America in 1970 a man strangled his wife because she put his morning newspaper on the wrong side of him at the breakfast table.

The Wallace case has been termed the 'motiveless murder'. This author has considerable doubt about that. Nobody commits murder without some sort of motive – even when as is the case of the serial killer, the reason could be a simple blood lust. There is no reason to doubt that in 1931 breakdown of marriage was as prevalent as it is today, but the procedure for divorce was more difficult and the cost relatively greater and the stigma more severe than is now the case. There was more incentive to present a placid front to the world. This outward veneer of peace and calm could disguise a turbulent undercurrent.

A feature of the husband and wife murder is the character of the husband. In the majority of criminal cases, defending counsel makes a point of stressing the previous good character of his client. This may or may not be a pertinent point. A clever and successful villain who boasts a previous good character may simply be skilful at having evaded detection in the past. But the defendant may have progressed from minor to more serious crimes, and it is important for the court to know if the offence charged is 'out of character' from what is known of the defendant. In cases of domestic murder, however, the accused frequently enjoys a previously genuinely good character, at least as far as the law is concerned. Devereux, Crippin and Ruxton were all mild men with no history of crime. They were men who had become encased in a situation they could no longer endure and adopted a desperate remedy. This point is of considerable importance in the Wallace case. For here was a man who had led a blameless life for 53 years, He was an insurance agent who had given faithful service for 16 years, although he had received no promotion.

With very little exception, his work colleagues and others who had known him spoke well of his character and personality, and his marriage by his own and most other accounts was a happy one. Could such a man have murdered his wife of nearly 17 years in a savage attack which involved a number of crushing blows to the head delivered with ferocious force? Sadly the history of this class of crime provides an affirmative answer. In many cases of murder the defendant, convicted on overwhelming evidence, has been spoken of by friends and family in the most creditable terms. Their reaction has been simply to refuse to believe the man that they know could have done such a thing.

So now let us take a look at this man who's life ended on such a mysterious and disastrous note, and at the woman who was his wife.

William Herbert Wallace was born in the town of Millom, Cumberland on 29 August 1878. His parents had three children, of which Wallace was the eldest. The family were working or more accurately lower middle-class, and Mr Wallace Senior combined the work of a printer with that of a part time agent for the Prudential Insurance Company. Wallace showed himself at school to be an intelligent pupil. He showed a particular interest in science and he retained this interest for the whole of his life, a fact which is indicated by the conversion of a room in his home at Wolverton Street into a miniature laboratory. He was spoken of as possessing an exceptional thirst for knowledge, mostly in the field of botany. There would seem to be little doubt that if he had had a more fortunate start in life William would have gone a great deal further than he did. But in the early part of the 20th century class mobility was much more restricted than it is today, and only a small minority of working-class boys who were bright enough to be of scholarship standard had any chance of getting to public school or university, and hence finding an entrance to the middle or upper middle class.

When Wallace was ten years old the family moved to Blackpool. The Wallace family at this time consisted of his parents Benjamin and Marjory Wallace, a younger sister named Jessie and his brother Joseph Edwin, who although two years younger bore a remarkable resemblance to William. It was then that Wallace suffered the first of those illnesses which were to blight his health and deeply influence the direction of his life. He was stricken with typhoid fever.

After leaving school at the age of 14 he became assistant to a linen draper in Barrow. He held this job for six years. Then he moved to Manchester and there, at the age of 20, worked for three years with a textile company. At both Barrow and Manchester Wallace entered hospital suffering from a kidney ailment. This was the disease which was to dog him the whole of his life and for which he never found an effective cure. It has been suggested that his medical condition had a considerable influence upon his psychological as well as physical, condition and may have been largely responsible for the final drama which engulfed him.

In 1902, Wallace made his bid for a more interesting and eventful life. At the age of 23 we find him on a ship bound for Calcutta. Once there he obtained work as a salesman in a trading company, but once again his kidney problems troubled him and further treatment during his two or three years in India failed to cure him. Wallace's next move may well have been influenced by the fact that his brother Joseph, now married, was in employment with the Chinese Government. William went on to Shanghai to join his brother and, again weakened by ill health, took a part time job as an advertising manager. Again he was operated on for his illness and once more the treatment was ineffective. Disappointed and dispirited William returned to England and in April 1907 his left kidney was removed.

Following his operation Wallace had a long convalescence. He then went to live in Harrogate and obtained a position as an agent for the Liberal Party. This was Wallace's only foray into politics and it didn't last very long. What did last was the start of his relationship with Julia, which culminated in their marriage in March 1914. After their marriage William and Julia moved to Liverpool where William became an agent for the Prudential Insurance Company, a position that he held for 16 years until Julia's tragic death. Wallace described his time in Harrogate as the happiest of his life and according to him, and the entries in his diaries, made both before and after his trial, his marriage was not merely successful but even blissful. That in short is the fairly mundane history of William Herbert Wallace.

Now let us take a look at the character of this unexceptional, but also rather strange, individual. It should be said right away that one should not go too far in seeking to infer from a man's personality or interests that these things in themselves advance the proposition that he is of the material that makes up a murderer. People of sound mind and perfectly good character sometimes have unusual hobbies. The reverse is also true, namely that the most apparently harmless people can commit terrible crimes. However, when there is a case of murder in which there is such a complete absence of direct evidence (as in this case), the nature, history and psychological make-up of the accused person has to be a relevant consideration.

As in other aspects of this baffling case there have been sharp disagreements between writers and criminologists about the character and personality of Wallace. The accounts given by people who knew him also differ. He has been variously described as 'charming and affable' and being 'a sour and disappointed man'. Let us see if these views can be reconciled, and if not, which is correct.

As a boy at school William was both intelligent and popular. In his early work as a linen draper's assistant in Barrow and with a textile company in Manchester nothing is known to his detriment. The same may be said for his employment in Calcutta and Shanghai. Only his poor health ended these activities. Similarly with his time as an agent for the Liberal party where reports confirm that he was both active and involved in the work of the party of his choice. In his final and longest occupation as an insurance agent his performance can be described as well nigh impeccable. As a door to door salesman selling and servicing policies he was hard working and conscientious and his book-keeping was perfect. There is not a word from any of his colleagues or superiors to indicate that he was anything other than an honest hard working employee.

Now let us consider the less favourable reaction of people who knew Wallace and his wife well. Much can be derived from the dossier prepared by Inspector Gold on Wallace's background. Gold worked on the investigation under Detective Superintendent Moore. He examined the house on the muder night and made a report on Wallace. Mrs Wilson, who had worked as a help at the Wallaces' home and who was also the matron of a police remand home, described Wallace as a man who appeared to have suffered a serious disappointment in life. Perhaps, having regard to William's constant setbacks through his kidney disease, not too much should be drawn from this. The words of Alfred Mather however, a retired Prudential Agent, are more significant. He had known Wallace for 12 years. He described his fellow agent as 'the most cool, calculating, despondent and soured man he had ever met'; one who was a 'bad tempered devil' who detested his work and thought it was beneath him to have become a mere insurance agent. He would not associate with fellow agents, possessing nauseating pride and a very morose manner. Mather was the only agent with whom Wallace would converse.

This judgement is so severe that it looks like the expression of personal animosity rather than an impartial assessment, but it was nonetheless significant. Dr Curwen the physician who regularly attended Wallace said in Gold's report 'he is a very reserved type of man and outside his business acquaintances and few members of the chess club he does not appear to have formed many friendships'. As against the above however there were voices raised in Wallace's favour. Joseph Crewe, a Prudential Supervisor, and Wallace's 'chief' spoke from a knowledge of over 12 years when he said 'he bears the highest character absolutely in every respect. To say that he is a kindly gentleman would be putting it mildly. No form of words would be too high praise for Wallace in that respect'.

Samuel Beattie, captain of the Liverpool central chess club which Wallace belonged to, considered that Wallace was a likeable man once one had broken through his reserve, while Mrs Ann Miller, a client, said that she had never met a nicer man. J T Fergusson who knew Wallace well called him 'a delightful fellow who was liked by all'.

What is one to make of these diverse views? Like so much else about the Wallace case there is uncertainty and ambiguity. What seems certain is that one is left with a taut and introverted man of suppressed emotion and pride on which he had little of substance to base it. A very mediocre achiever who had a secret longing to have done much better in life and as such struggled inwardly against a nagging sense of inadequacy. But this does not make a man a potential murderer.

Let us now turn our attention to Julia Wallace. Little is known about her history prior to her coming into Wallace's life, and certainly little or nothing that has any relevance to the enquiry into her murder. She was one of six children of William George Dennis, whom she said was a veterinary surgeon, and his French born wife Aimee. The mother died when Julia was 10. There is some uncertainty about her age, but Julia was 52 at the time of her death and therefore in her thirties at the time of her marriage. She was a gifted woman, something of which her husband certainly appeared to be proud. She spoke fluent French, played the piano very competently and painted in water colours. But she was shy by nature and like her husband suffered from fragile health. Her photograph, taken at an unknown date after her marriage, shows a face with a wan smile and sad eyes. It is not a happy face and like William, she seems to betray a certain sense of resignation, even disillusionment with life.

Nevertheless some of the wilder assertions about her, for example that she had a dubious past and was being blackmailed by a former lover, appear entirely without foundation in fact. The absence of any member of her family from the marriage would possibly indicate that they disapproved of her union with William. There were no children of the match but this does not seem to have been a problem for either of them, and to make a suggestion, as has been done, that this was a cause of friction is pure supposition. The air of mystery which hangs about William and Julia as individuals is also an element in their marriage. Yet although things may not have been as idyllic as Wallace maintained, the majority view was certainly that their married life was peaceful and untroubled. A placid if not formative companionship. Yet here also there have been voices who express doubts.

Mrs Wilson has said that when she was at the Wallace home nursing William, Julia did not seem to have any wish to keep the house clean, she did not appear to have any enthusiasm for anything. She did, however, suffer from recurrent chest trouble and also from depression. This may well have affected her capacity for housework. Julia was a regular member of the congregation at the Holy Trinity Catholic Church nearby, while Wallace himself was an agnostic. However this fact, like the absence of children, presented no apparent problem. Dr Curwen, who was the couple's regular doctor did not think that they enjoyed the happy and harmonious relationship that outsiders supposed. Yet Wallace's entries into his diaries during the time after his release are so full of expressions of devotion that it is difficult to believe they are not sincere.

That for June 6 1931:

... my dear Julia is seldom out of my thoughts and now I am on my own I now realise the fight I am going to have with battle against loneliness and desolation, Julia, Julia how can I do without you, the anguish in my soul rises up and distils itself in tears which I cannot hold back.

September 8 1931:

The last few days I have been desperately thinking of my dear Julia. I'm afraid this will be a very lonely winter for me. I seem to miss her more and more and cannot drive the thought of her cruel end out of my mind".

March 20 1932:

Today I have been very much depressed, full of grief and tears, Julia, Julia my dear, why were you taken from me?

At his trial Wallace was questioned by his counsel Roland Oliver KC about his relationship with Julia:

OLIVER: What were your relations with your wife?

WALLACE: What I should describe as perfect.

OLIVER: Is there anyone in the world who could take the place of your wife in your life?

WALLACE: No there is not.

OLIVER: Have you got anyone to live with now?

WALLACE: No.

OLIVER: Or to live for?

WALLACE: No.

Much has been said about the hobbies of Wallace. The contrast has been drawn between his intellectual interests and his mundane existence. This is a situation typical of a lively but untrained mind. It not being his destiny to pursue one of the learned professions, he had to content himself with the amateurish dabbling into subjects far beyond his normal horizons. These interests were varied: experiments in chemistry; chess, at which he was no better than average; playing the violin, at which he was a complete novice, and the study of Stoicism. Much has been made of his addiction to chess. It has even been suggested that this indicates a scheming, duplicitous mind well capable of planning the 'perfect murder'. In the view of this writer such nonsense may well be dispensed with in the study of this baffling case. Stoicism however, is a different matter. It has been said that our thoughts are what we are. There is an element of truth in the proposition that a man's beliefs at least contribute to, if not determine, his actions. Wallace's air of detachment, almost unconcern, at the scene of his wife's murder, during his detention and trial and indeed throughout his entire ordeal impresses some observers as unnatural. A point of this was made at his trial, and it would seem that the cool, shrewd manner in which he gave evidence made a poor impression on the jury. His gift for suppressing his emotions were in keeping with the Stoic philosophy, and no doubt related to it.

Let us consider Stoicism and its teaching, bearing in mind that Wallace's favourite and most treasured work was *The Meditations of Marcus Aurelius*. The Roman Emperor who embraced Stoicism in the second century AD. Stoicism was the philosophy founded by Zeno of Citium and then developed by Ceanthes and Crysippus. It was so named after the Stoae Poikite or Painted Porch, which was the place in Athens where the philosophers of the Stoic school taught. Emperor of Rome Marcus Aurelius was the last figure in the ancient world to adopt its teachings, but the influence of its doctrines survived and the term stoic is used to this day to describe the acceptance of misfortune without complaint. For the Stoics, reason was prominent in understanding the world as a whole, both as applied to human behaviour and in the divinely ordered cosmos. Stoicism was not atheistic, and has made a contribution to both Neoplatonic and Christian thought. Stoic philosophy has a very strong element of of resignation and fatalism. For example, Stoic philosophers maintained that if a perfectly wise and virtuous man saw his child in danger of drowning he would try to save it, but that if he failed he would accept that, without feeling distress or pity and without his happiness being diminished. Since everything that happens is governed by divine providence his failure must have been for the best, even if he could not understand why. Moreover, moral virtue is the only good and wickedness is the only evil. So the child's death was not in itself an evil.

Furthermore, since moral virtue is the only good, and by being perfectly virtuous the wise man may well have done, by definition, the best he could, there is nothing for him to regret. The Stoics made 'following nature' the centre of their ethics, explaining the development of moral awareness by the individual's progressive realisation of what is naturally appropriate for him. The Stoics taught that all that matters is our attempts to do what is right; health and wealth are naturally preferable to sickness and poverty, and we should pursue them if we do not wrong others thereby, but achieving them is beyond our control. The wise man while doing the best he can in the circumstances as he sees them, is prepared to accept the eventual outcome as the will of providence, and thus he alone is free. The Stoic is like an archer, who cares less about actually hitting the target than about doing his best to hit it, and his wisdom includes understanding the difference between what is in his favour and what is not. Only the perfectly wise man is good, and he is very rare. All others are both mad and bad, and all crimes are equal.

Emotions such as distress, pity (which is a species of distress) and fear, which reflect a false judgement about what is evil, are to be avoided (as also are those which reflect a false judgement about what is good such as a love of honour or riches). The Stoics, however could not adequately explain why, when virtue was the only good, divine providence should bring it about that almost everyone is bad. Christianity provided the answer to this problem with the doctrine of original sin, but perhaps what doomed Stoicism was its lack of compassion. It came close to providing escape from a sense of responsibility. The suppression of human emotion is a dangerous exercise. It may involve actions which are only possible when normal human sensitivity has been laid aside. Did the study of Stoicism have this effect on Wallace? We shall never know the answer to this question for certain.

CHAPTER THREE

WHO IS QUALTROUGH?

The feature of the Wallace case which makes it so unique in the history of crime is that it is the only occasion on which a telephone call has been the instrument of murder. It has been almost universally agreed by criminologists and other students of this strange case, and also by those engaged on both sides in the trial, that the caller was the murderer. The simple issue in the case was and is – who made the phone call? Was it William Wallace or somebody else? There was a wide area of agreed facts. The case formed largely on the interpretation of these facts. There has rarely been a case of murder in which the known facts were open to such a widely different interpretation. That is why the case for the prosecution rested mainly, if not entirely, on circumstantial rather than direct evidence.

On the evening of 19 January 1931 at about 7.15pm William Wallace set out to play in a competition at the chess club to which he belonged: The Central Chess Club which met at Liverpool's City Café. His decision to go was spontaneous because his wife Julia had been unwell and he had intended to stay with her that evening. However, since her condition had improved he changed his mind and resolved to go. Wallace's plan was to catch a tram from Belmont Road to the café at 21 North John Street in Liverpool. 400 yards from Wallace's house in Wolverton Street in the district of Anfield stood a telephone box at the junction of Breck Road and Rochester Road. At 7.15pm someone entered this box and made a phone call which was the preliminary to murder.

According to Wallace, having left home he walked along Richmond Park and then, by his own account, turned into Breck Road at the corner of Trinity Church, then down Breck Road and left along Belmont Road to the tram stop. Having reached his destination Wallace was seen at the chess club at 7.45pm or thereabouts. Before Wallace arrived at the club a telephone call had been received. The caller asked if Wallace was there. Told that he had not yet arrived he said he could not ring back and asked to leave a message. The message which was passed on to Wallace by Samuel Beattie, the captain of the club, was that a man calling himself Qualtrough wanted Wallace to visit him the following evening on a matter which concerned Wallace's business, namely insurance. The address which Qualtrough gave was 25 Menlove Gardens East, Mossley Hill.

Wallace was puzzled. He said he had never heard of anyone of that name before, nor did he know the address. Wallace, after some discussion with other members of the club decided to go. In fact both the name and the address were fictitious. Next day after he had completed his rounds as an insurance agent, Wallace set off for his appointment with Qualtrough. He took a tram to Menlove Avenue and searched unsuccessfully for Menlove Gardens East. After asking directions from a number of people he abandoned the search and returned home. There he discovered the body of his wife, lying on the floor of the front parlour with her head beaten in by a number of ferocious blows with a blunt instrument. The police were summoned and the investigation began. In due course Wallace himself was accused of the crime. It was alleged that Wallace himself had made the phone call, calling himself Qualtrough and speaking in a disguised voice; that he gave a false address and thus provided himself with an alibi, and that by the time he left his house he had already murdered his wife. At his trial for murder the jury convicted him after a retirement of only one hour. Wallace appealed to the Court of Criminal Appeal. The court with, an unprecedented judgement, overturned the verdict of the jury and Wallace was released. There was considerable prejudice against Wallace by people in the neighbourhood where he lived and worked, as a result of which he was obliged to retire. Two years later he died and was buried next to his wife. This is the barest outline of one of the most perplexing cases in English legal history.

The Wallace case has been variously termed the 'perfect murder', 'unbeatable' and an example of planning so brilliant that the murderer, whoever he was, must have been something of a genius. This author will seek to show that none of these descriptions are appropriate. It was not a prefect murder and the man who committed it was far from being a genius. It will also be demonstrated in this work what the most likely solution really is. The events which we shall be examining occurred over two days – the 19th and 20th January 1931. Because alternative suggestions have been made since that time as to the guilt or innocence of William Wallace we shall consider these and also enquire into the possibility of there being another culprit. Finally, this author will submit what must be the true answer to a mystery which has tested and taxed the intelligence of some of the best students of crime.

Of course it is not incumbent on the defence in a murder trial to prove that somebody other than the accused committed the crime. That important principle applied especially in the case of Wallace. This was so for two reasons. First, in the case of a wife being murdered, suspicion, not unnaturally, tends to settle on the husband. Secondly, in this particular case, the victim was a quiet unoffending middle aged lady who had no known enemies. Moreover there were no signs of a break in at 29 Wolverton Street and Julia Wallace had firm instructions from her husband not to admit anyone into their home who was not a known friend. At the subsequent trial Mr Justice Wright, a judge of great distinction, was careful to warn the jury of this important rule of English criminal law. This is so important to bear in mind as we wend our way through this drama that we should hear and ponder the words of the judge:

> The real test of the value of circumstantial evidence is; Does it exclude other theories or possibilities? If you cannot put the evidence against the accused man beyond a possibility and nothing more, if that is a probability which is not inconsistent with there being other reasonable possibilities, then it is impossible for a jury to say: We are satisfied beyond reasonable doubt that the charge is made against the accused man. A man cannot be convicted for any crime, least of all murder, merely on possibilities, unless they are so strong as to amount to be a reasonable certainty. If you have other possibilities, a jury would not and, I believe ought not, to come to the conclusion that the charge is established.

Then follow these significant words:

> The question is not who did this crime? The question is: Did the prisoner do it? Or rather, to put it more accurately: Is it proved to your reasonable satisfaction and beyond all reasonable doubt that the prisoner did it? It is a fallacy to say "if the prisoner did not do it, who did? It is a fallacy to look at it and say: "It is very difficult to think the prisoner did not do it"; and it may be equally difficult to think the prisoner did do it; The prosecution have to discharge the onus cast upon them of establishing the guilt of the prisoner and must go far beyond suspicion or surmise, or even probability; unless the probability is such as to amount to a practical certainty; and where a jury is considering circumstantial evidence, they must always bear these considerations in mind, and must not be led by any extraneous considerations to act upon what cannot be regarded as – well I cannot say mere suspicion – but cannot be regarded as establishing beyond peradventure, beyond all reasonable doubt, the guilt of the accused man.

The three phases, taken in chronological order, of events on 19 January are: first, Wallace's walk from his house at 29 Wolverton Street to the means of transportation to the chess club; second, the mystery telephone call; and thirdly, Wallace's reactions when informed at the club of the message which had been left for him by Qualtrough.

Let us therefore look closely at Wallace's movements on the evening of 19 January. There are two important factors to take into account. These are, first, that he knew the Anfield district as well as anyone could. For years he had been a door to door insurance salesman and had numerous clients in the vicinity. This was made clear at his trial in answer to questions from his counsel Roland Oliver KC:

OLIVER: What was your round, geographically? In Liverpool; how big a circle did you cover in your district?

WALLACE: I can hardly describe it in terms of area; it was a fairly considerable area.

OLIVER: Would your work take you more or less to a good many places?

WALLACE: Yes I think altogether I would have something like five hundred and sixty calls to make each week, approximately.

OLIVER: I take it you must have been fairly well known as a rounds man in the district?

WALLACE: Very well known. These answers speak for themselves on that matter.

The second important point is that Wallace's account of his journey to the chess club is supported by his own uncorroborated evidence alone. This is highly significant as to the times and the route. As to both of these aspects of the case it is, again, of interest to look at Wallace's evidence at the trial.

OLIVER: We know you were due to go and play a match of chess. I will take this as shortly as I can. What time did you leave your house to go to the chess club?

WALLACE: As near as I can tell you, about a quarter past seven.

OLIVER: That is the time you gave the police near the event?

WALLACE: Yes.

OLIVER: How did you go there, by what method? I do not want the whole route, but did you walk or go by tram or how?

WALLACE: I walked up Richmond Park, turned the corner by the church and up Belmont Road and caught a tram.

OLIVER: It has been suggested that you used the telephone box to telephone a message to yourself. Is there a word of truth in that?

WALLACE: Absolutely none.

Dealing with the question of time, it has to be asked whether Wallace gave an accurate account of the time at which he left home. Much has been made of the fact by writers who have leaned towards the innocence of Wallace, that since the telephone call was logged by the operator at 7.15pm, he would not have had the time to have reached the phone box and made the mystery call. However the words of Wallace as the trial were "as near as I can tell you, about quarter past seven". This element of vagueness while giving the appearance of being quite genuine, allows for a margin, which, even if only being a matter of a few minutes, would have given him ample time, at a brisk walk to reach the telephone kiosk in time to make the 7.15pm call. It was not disputed that four minutes would have been adequate. If Wallace had turned right instead of left, as he asserted, at the corner of Richmond Park and Breck Road, this would have brought him very swiftly to the telephone kiosk in question. This would have only involved a minor deviation from the route which he admitted having taken. But was he being truthful?

Wallace was keen to get to the city café in time for his game. The acknowledged time at the club for start of play was 7.45pm. Why then did he not take the much shorter route from Wolverton Street, across Richmond Park, past the church institute, left into Castlewood Road and down to Belmont Road which would have brought him to the tram stop he wanted, but in half the time. Was it because this route was nowhere near the telephone box where Qualtrough made his call? Somewhat surprisingly this question was not taken up by Edward Hemmerde, Counsel for the Crown, in his cross examination at the trial.

In her interesting contribution to *The Anatomy of Murder* (The Bodley Head, 1936) Dorothy L Sayers poses the theory that on the night of 19 January the man who we shall call for convenience by his fictitious name of 'Qualtrough' was keeping observation on 29 Wolverton Street for the purpose of seeing when Wallace left the house. He then went to the telephone box and when he saw Wallace pass the box he made his call to the city café, leaving his message prior to Wallace's arrival. It seems to this author that this proposition apart from being pure supposition, is full of improbabilities. First, the house where Wallace and his wife lived had two entrances. One onto Wolverton Street and the other through a yard at the back of the house onto a passageway. It would have been difficult, if not impossible for a watcher to keep in view both at the same time, particularly since he would not know from which one Wallace was going to exit. Nor would he have known whether Wallace would go along Richmond Park or take the shorter route to Belmont Road down Castlewood Road. Secondly, anyone hanging about on a dark night may well arouse suspicion, especially so since the area was under police observation following several burglaries in the neighbourhood. Wallace himself admitted these points when put to him at his trial by Hemmerde in cross examination.

> HEMMERDE: Then he rang you at 7.15 or 7.20, and without knowing you would ever get the message, and without ever knowing you would go to Menlove Gardens East, apparently he was ready waiting for your departure the next night?
>
> WALLACE: It would look like it.
>
> HEMMERDE: Did it ever occur to you that he would have to watch both doors front and back?

WALLACE: No, it did not.

Thirdly, Miss Sayers says that Wallace was a regular attendant at the chess club. In fact he was a spasmodic attender who had failed to keep several appointments. Fourthly, it is apparent from the message that the knowledge of the watcher was that Wallace was an insurance agent. This rules out a casual intruder as the murderer and as to the possibility of a friend or colleague of Wallace being "Qualtrough" we have this extract from his trial:

HEMMERDE (cross examination): As far as you know she had no enemies at all?

WALLACE: I do not think she had a single one.

HEMMERDE: And although you gave certain names to the police of persons she might have admitted, is there one of them against whom you have the slightest suspicion of having committed this offence?

WALLACE: No.

Fifthly, Wallace did not pass the telephone box. An innocent Wallace would have turned left at the junction of Richmond Park and Breck Road and hence it would have been difficult if not impossible to see from the telephone box at the junction of Breck Road and Rochester Road, on a dark night. The distance was some 500 feet from the telephone box to the church corner. Finally, the telephone box was in a quiet corner of the town and only lit by a lamp from outside. It was ideal for someone who wanted to conceal his identity from persons who might know him as a familiar figure in the neighbourhood.

In order that the case against Wallace for the murder of his wife Julia be proved it was necessary for the Crown to prove two things: First, that he was Qualtrough and secondly that his was the hand that struck her down. There was no direct evidence; no eyewitnesses, no fingerprints, no scientific data and no admissions. The only chance which the Crown had of proving their case was to present such an accumulation of circumstantial evidence that a jury would be able to say that no intelligent person could come to any other conclusion but that Wallace was guilty. This is frequently a difficult task for the prosecution. It was so in this case. The tactic of the defence in such a situation is to attack each element of the testimony given by the prosecution witnesses so that the eventual position sometimes amounts to the upshot that zero, plus zero, plus zero equals zero. An able and experienced defending counsel avoids direct confrontation with the Crown witnesses. He is not expected to disprove his opponent's case. His correct strategy is to undermine it and so create a doubt in the minds of the jury.

With this in mind we shall shortly examine the nature and contents of the telephone call which was the catalyst to murder. First, let us investigate the completion of Wallace's journey to the chess club. Once again remember we have only the uncorroborated account of Wallace himself. The police, in their enthusiasm to solve their baffling problem, failed to make any enquiry as to which tram Wallace took to got to the chess club or from which stop. This might have shown Wallace to be a liar and almost certainly the killer of his wife or it could have cleared him. Did Wallace really as he claimed, turn down into Breck Road and then go up Belmont Road, and there catch a tram? Or did he enter the telephone box, make the call and then board a tram at the stop opposite the box.

Writers who have favoured the idea of Wallace being innocent have emphasised the likelihood that Wallace could not have been Qualtrough because there would not have been sufficient time for him to have completed the phone call and made his arrival at the club in time for his game of chess, which was scheduled to commence at 7.45pm. This ignores two considerations. First, the uncertainty of witnesses as to the time Wallace arrived at the club. Samuel Beattie asked by Hemmerde in cross examination:

HEMMERDE: Rather later did you see the accused in the café?

BEATTIE: I did.

HEMMERDE: About what time was that?

BEATTIE: About half an hour after I had received the message, say a quarter to eight.

HEMMERDE: Had you seen him come in?

BEATTIE: I had not.

James Cairns was equally vague:

HEMMERDE: What time did the accused arrive?

CAIRNS: I should think about 7.45.

If Wallace had completed his telephone conversation at around 7.19pm and then taken a tram taking 21 minutes to the City Café in North John Street he would have arrived at the club only a minute or two after 7.45pm, when play was due to begin.

The second point has been raised by James Murphy in his very thorough work in the subject *The Murder of Julia Wallace*, Murphy quotes Wallace's first statement to the police at Anfield Bridewell made just before midnight on the night of the murder. Murphy points out that buses number 10 and 11 stopped at a bus stop near the tram stop opposite the telephone kiosk, either of which would have taken Wallace to North John Street where the chess club was situated. Wallace sometimes used buses as well as trams and on the 19 January may well have thought that this would take him to the chess club more quickly.

Perhaps if Roland Oliver KC had felt that there was anything of substance in this point he would have used it to Wallace's advantage at his trial. He did not. The question was not raised by either side. Once again, as with other issues in this strange case, we are in the realm of supposition.

Now let us examine the all-important phone call itself which was made by Qualtrough – we shall call him, whoever he was, by the name he gave to Beattie. There are four aspects which should be closely noted. First, the hiatus which caused the call to be logged by the operator; secondly the words used by the caller; thirdly the caller's voice; and fourthly, the response of Wallace when the message was passed on to him.

The type of telephone in use in 1931 was of the older kind which persisted until some years after the Second World War. The procedure was to enter the kiosk, lift the receiver, dial the required number and place the coins in the coin box. When an answer was forthcoming one pressed button A and was connected to the person on the other end of the line. When connection was made and button A was pressed the coins fell and could not be retrieved. If, notwithstanding a ringing at the other end, there was no reply one pressed button B and the money was returned. It is quite extraordinary that in the transcript of the trial given by W F Wyndham-Brown in his book *The Trial of William Herbert Wallace* (Gollancz, 1933) the evidence given is both inadequate and inaccurate. Leslie Heaton called by the prosecution:

> I am a telephone electrician. There is a telephone box at the junction of Rochester Road and Breckfield Road, Anfield. There is a telephone-call box in the public library in Breck Road. There are several other call-boxes in that district.
>
> Mr Justice Wright: Public ones?
>
> Heaton: Yes, but they are not as public as this one in as much as the kiosk is fitted on a site of it's own, and the other call-boxes are on enclosed premises.
>
> Counsel for the Crown: They are in the library or in shops?
>
> Heaton: Yes.

The only question put by Roland Oliver KC for the defence to Heaton related to the lighting at the kiosk. In answer to a question by the judge Heaton explained that the only lighting came from a lamp outside. The all-important fact that, following the Qualtrough complaint about his difficulty in getting through, the telephone engineer was sent to examine the mechanism was not mentioned. Nor was the fact that he found a fault in the mechanism which he repaired. In her book *Two studies of crime* (Macmillan, 1970) Yseult Bridges quotes the official record of the incident.

> When the caller was first plugged through he received no answer, necessitating a second call. He complained to the operator of not being put through properly in the first place, and after some conversation the supervisor refunded the two pence he had paid for the second call. These two different operators testified that the man who booked the call had 'an ordinary voice and was rather polite'.

Bridges also points out that in the Anfield area calls from a public telephone were automatically recorded at the exchange, and that operators used manual methods. In Wyndham-Brown's transcript of the evidence only one operator appears, Lillian Martha Kelly. In fact three operators were involved. The sequence of events was as follows. The first operator was Louise Alfreds. She received a call from a male voice and made the connection with the chess club, the number being Bank 3581. Nothing seems to have come of that call, indicating a fault with the phone mechanism. A few minutes later another operator Lillian Kelly heard the voice of the caller saying 'Operator, I have pressed button A but I have not had my correspondent yet'. Kelly told the caller to press button B and saw the red light on her console which indicated that he had done so and that the money had been refunded. Kelly then tried to get Bank 3581, but failed, again indicating there was a fault. The matter was then referred to the supervisor Annie Robertson. She spoke to the caller who explained the difficulties. Robertson then tried Bank 3581 without success. Another indication of the fault. At 7.20pm Kelly put through the call which was taken by Gladys Harley at the club. Harley later insisted that the telephone had not rung prior to that last call. Again, showing clearly that there was a fault in the mechanism.

It has been suggested on behalf of Wallace that Qualtrough was a man who had a grudge against the latter and deliberately confused the telephone conversation with the operators in order to facilitate the identification of the number and position of the kiosk. This theory would seem to this author to border on the absurd. That anyone with a complaint against Wallace should give effect to this by gaining access to his house and beating out the brains of this innocent and unoffending wife strains credulity beyond limits. In any event, providing Wallace with an alibi would be calculated to have the opposite effect.

Furthermore, the reason why the call was logged was because a fault was reported. At no time did Qualtrough disclose to the operator where he was phoning from. Surely the more likely explanation is that Qualtrough's plan did not take into account the unexpected.

The case for the Crown was that Qualtrough was in fact Wallace himself and that when he rang the club he spoke with a disguised voice, he did so in order to provide himself with an alibi to cover the time when his wife was murdered – by himself. It is worth noting that all three operators, and Gladys Harley who took the call at the club described the caller as having quite an ordinary voice. Gladys Harley did however say it seemed like the voice of an 'elderly gentleman'. This would seem to rule out anyone who was young or 'youngish'. Samuel Beattie, the captain of the chess club, gave an efficient and more positive account. Asked by counsel what sort of voice it was replied: 'A strong voice, a rather gruff voice'. The judge asked him 'you used the words (to the police) it was a confident voice'. Beattie said 'yes' in answer to the question; 'it was a confident voice, sure of himself'. This discrepancy between the accounts given by the telephone operators and the café waitress on the one hand and Beattie on the other tends to support he view that 'Qualtrough' disguised his voice when speaking to the club captain. Why should he do this? Surely because he had no fear of being recognised by the girls but knew that his normal voice was familiar to members of the club. This can only mean that he was either a member of, or a frequent visitor to, the City Café.

At the trial Roland Oliver KC for Wallace took a considerable risk when he cross-examined Beattie:

OLIVER: So far as you could judge, was it a natural voice?

BEATTIE: That is difficult to judge.

OLIVER: I know it is, but did it occur to you that it was not a natural voice at the time?

BEATTIE: No. I had no reason for thinking that.

OLIVER: Do you know Mr Wallace's voice well?

BEATTIE: Yes.

OLIVER: Did it occur to you that it was anything like his voice?

BEATTIE: Certainly not.

OLIVER: Does it occur to you now it was anything like his voice?

BEATTIE: It would be a great stretch of the imagination for me to say it was anything like that.

It must be remembered that audibility was much less perfect on the telephone in 1931 than it is today. It should also be borne in mind that to disguise a voice it is not necessary to affect a particular accent. As change of emphasis or of volume may suffice.

Now let us consider the words which were spoken by 'Qualtrough' when he first spoke to Gladys Harley. He enquired 'Is that the central chess club?'

On being told that it was he said 'Is Mr Wallace there?' These are arguably the words of someone who expected Wallace to be there. Otherwise he might have said something like: 'Do you know if Mr Wallace will be at the club this evening?' That narrows the field of possible callers to an individual who had watched Wallace's movements on his journey to the café – or to Wallace himself. It is important here to examine the transcript of the trial on this point:

OLIVER: I am interested in the voice that addressed you on the telephone on this particular evening. How much conversation did you have with it? Could you reproduce the conversation for us, do you think?

BEATTIE: Yes partly. I can give you an idea of the conversation.

OLIVER: The part I am interested in particularly is the part in which the voice told you about the business, whatever it was. Can you remember what the voice said about that?

BEATTIE: Yes. I told him that Mr Wallace was coming to the club that night and that he would be there shortly, would he ring up again. He said no I am too busy; I have got my girl's twenty-first birthday on, and I want to see Mr Wallace on a matter of business; it is something in the nature of his business.

OLIVER: Something in the nature of his business, coupled with a reference to his daughter?

BEATTIE: That was the reason he was not able to phone Mr Wallace himself later that night, because he was too busy with his girl's twenty-first birthday .

There are three things of significance about this passage of conversation. First, the caller knew the profession of Wallace. Bear in mind that in his second statement to the police Wallace gave them the names of 14 men who would have been admitted to the house by Mrs Wallace in his absence. Yet he affirmed at the time, and later at the trial that there was not one of them he would suspect of murdering her. And there were no signs of the house having been broken into at the time of the murder. Again, this greatly narrows the field of possible suspects, One only was subsequently targeted by some writers, but this was many years later and the person concerned, Richard Gordon Parry, was thoroughly investigated by the police at the time. The accusation against Parry will be dealt with later in this work. Secondly, the caller was anxious to avoid at all costs calling again later. This was no doubt, either because he did not wish to speak with Wallace himself, or because Qualtrough was indeed Wallace and it would be impossible for him to call again. Lastly, the extraordinary excuse that he could not phone later because he was involved with his daughter's 21st birthday party should surely have alerted Wallace to the bogus nature of the message.

Samuel Beattie delivered the telephone message to Wallace, when he was playing chess with a member named McCartney, that a man calling himself Qualtrough wanted Wallace to call on him the following evening at 7.30pm at 25 Menlove Gardens East. Wallace expressed himself as mystified by both the name and the address. Told by Beattie that it was a bad place to be knocking about at night Wallace replied that he 'belonged to Liverpool' and had a 'scotch tongue' in his head. Wallace wrote the address down in his diary.

Wallace left the City Café that night at 10.20pm with Caird, who beside being a fellow member of the club was a friend of some years standing. Wallace and Caird caught a tram and alighted at the stop near St Margaret's Church in Belmont Road. They then followed the route which was the most direct to Caird's house in Letchworth Street. This involved walking along Castlewood Road into Letchworth Street, and then, for Wallace, across Richmond Park and into the passage that led to his home at 29 Wolverton Street. It is not be missed that this way, which was clearly familiar to Wallace, would have been much the quickest route to the chess club, but *on the way to* the club he chose a much longer itinerary, one which took him near to the telephone kiosk.

During the walk home with Caird the subject of Qualtrough again came up Wallace said 'it's a funny name, I have never heard a name like that before, have you?' Wallace then went home, and that concluded events on 19 January.

CHAPTER FOUR

THE HOUSE THAT WASN'T THERE

Writers who favour the view that Wallace was innocent regard his search for 25 Menlove Gardens East as a genuine quest for the whereabouts of that house, and its apparent occupant R M Qualtrough. They consider that his frequent requests for assistance were understandable for a man who was not familiar with the district.

The police however, came to a very different conclusion. They were certain that Wallace, having brutally murdered his wife, was putting into effect the false alibi for which he had laid the basis by his telephone call to the chess club, and that his constant asking for directions was intended to provide himself with witnesses in the event of his ever being brought to trial. This author does not wish to impose his own opinion on the reader, but rather to let him make up his own mind. However, there are certain elements in Wallace's conduct which arouse suspicion to say the least.

First, it should be noted that Wallace's own account of his movements up to the time when he boarded the first tram at 7.06 or 7.10pm is completely uncorroborated. This applies to the time at which he said he left the house, namely 6.45pm. Surprisingly, Wallace's evidence on these points was accepted without challenge. However, in his evidence in chief at the trial, Wallace was asked by his counsel, Roland Oliver: 'When you went out, was your wife alive?' He replied 'Certainly'. He was then asked: 'Did she come with you?' The answer was 'Yes'.

OLIVER: Tell us exactly how far she came, as far as you can remember.

WALLACE: She came down the back yard as far as the back yard door and I left her standing there, with an instruction to her to bolt the door after me. That was our usual practice.

OLIVER: Do you remember now whether she bolted it? Did you hear her bolt it?

WALLACE: I did not.

OLIVER: The police officer Williams says you told him she walked some of the way down the entry with you and then went back, and you heard her bolt the door. Is that right?

WALLACE: No.

That is a discrepancy which may or may not be important. Wallace after some hesitation, left the house to search for the non-existent address.

He went by the shorter route to Belmont Road to board his tram, rather than the longer way he had walked the day before when going to the chess club. Earlier in the day Wallace had completed his usual rounds. However, in a piece of evidence which may well have significance, police constable James Rothwell reports seeing Wallace, looking very upset at 3.30pm. The transcript of the trial reads:

HEMMERDE (CROWN COUNSEL): How was he dressed?

ROTHWELL: He was dressed in a tweed suit, and a light brown raincoat, a mackintosh.

MR JUSTICE WRIGHT: A raincoat?

ROTHWELL: Yes, my Lord.

HEMMERDE: What was he doing? Did you notice anything about him?

ROTHWELL: His face was haggard and drawn, and he was very distressed, unusually distressed.

HEMMERDE: What signs of distress did he show?

ROTHEWELL: He was dabbing his eye with his coat sleeve, and he appeared to me as if he had been crying.

HEMMERDE: Have you ever seen him like that before?

ROTHWELL: I have never seen him like that before.

HEMMERDE: Were you quite close to him?

ROTHWELL: Quite close to him, I passed him.

Roland Oliver, for the defence, adopted a tactic which is not unusual for defending counsel when confronted with a potentially damaging piece of evidence. That is, to put to the witness an alternative explanation. If the witness, not wishing to appear unreasonable or biased, agrees, then the impact upon the jury is diminished. If the witness does not agree he or she appears biased.

OLIVER: You did not take any notice of this until after you heard there had been a murder?

ROTHWELL: I did take notice of it when I see him coming along the road.

OLIVER: You did not say anything about it until after you had heard there had been a murder?

ROTHWELL: Yes.

OLIVER: I wonder if it occurred to you that your eyes could water in the cold. Has that happened to you?

ROTHWELL: Yes. It is quite possible.

OLIVER: What I am suggesting to you is that you are mistaken in thinking that the signs you saw were signs of distress occasioned by committing a crime?

ROTHWELL: No. I do not think so.

OLIVER: Although you never spoke to him?

ROTHWELL: He gave me that impression, as if he had suffered from some bereavement.

OLIVER: If I were to call about twenty five people who saw him that afternoon about that time, or round about that time, and they said he was just as usual, would you say they had made a mistake?

ROTHWELL: No. I should stick to my opinion.

In this latter passage, counsel refers to witnesses he has not called in evidence and has no intention of doing so. He is telling the jury what they would say if called. This comes very close to counsel giving evidence himself, it should also be borne in mind that Wallace was capable of masking his emotions. That is clear from his conduct after the discovery of Julia's body. PC Rothwell was an observant and trained officer who had known Wallace for two years. No doubt that he had seen him before many times, yet he was convinced that Wallace was in a state of distress. This is something which any student of the case should ponder. It cannot be brushed aside. What had occurred between Wallace and his wife to cause such signs of grief?

The next question that can usefully be asked is: Why didn't Wallace make enquiries of his own before setting out on what proved to be a 'wild goose hunt?' It seems extraordinary that an insurance agent who made his living on the streets should not have a directory of his own. In his evidence Wallace described his working district as 'a fairly considerable area'. Asked would your work take you more or less round to a good many places? He replied 'Yes, I think altogether I would have something like five hundred and sixty calls to make each week, approximately'. Even more inexplicable is the fact that he made no effort to consult a directory, which he could have obtained at the library near his home, or to telephone his supervisor, Joseph Crewe at Mossley Hill, who lived in the very district he was to visit. Even a quick call to the local police station might have saved him a lot of walking and many fruitless requests.

Having boarded a number 4 tram, Wallace spoke to the conductor Thomas Phillips and the ticket inspector Edward Angus. Phillips said that before Wallace got on the car he asked if it went to Menlove Gardens East. Phillips relied that it did not, but that he could get a number 5, 5A, 5W or a number 7. Wallace got on the tram and told Phillips that he was a stranger in the district, and that he had some important business or calls and that he wanted Menlove Gardens East. When Phillips was collecting fares Wallace said to him: 'You won't forget mister, I want Menlove Gardens East'. When Phillips was descending from the top deck Wallace again spoke to him about

Menlove Gardens East, and was told to change at Penny Lane. That made it three times that Wallace asked for that address. When ticket inspector Angus approached Wallace the latter said again that he wanted Menlove Gardens East. Having changed to a 5A tram Wallace asked tram conductor Arthur Thompson to put him off at Menlove Gardens East. Thompson directed him to Menlove Gardens West. Wallace again said he was a complete stranger in that area. James Murphy in *The Murder of Julia Wallace* writes:

> This was an obvious lie: as he alighted at Menlove Gardens West, ahead was Green Lane, where his superintendent Crewe lived, and further on, the entrance to Calderstones Park, where he had taken Julia many times. Wallace was not a stranger to that area of Liverpool.

Wallace then called at 25 Menlove Gardens West and spoke to the occupant, Katie Mather, who told him that there was nobody named Qualtrough living at that address. Wallace then returned to Menlove Avenue where he spoke to a stranger who was unable to help him. Wallace told the court at his trial that he found himself in Green Lane where his superintendent Joseph Crewe lived. It should be noted here that he had in the past visited Crewe's house a number of times, and the impression he gave the court that he was unfamiliar with Green Lane rings very hollow. It should also be noted that in none of his four statements to the police had he mentioned that he had tried to contact Crewe at his home but that there was no reply to his attempts.

The next person Wallace approached was police constable James Edward Sargent who was on duty at the junction of Green Lane and Allerton Road. Sargent's answer in his examination in chief are important in the case as will be seen from the transcript:

HEMMERDE: When you were there did someone come up to you?

SARGENT: The accused.

HEMMERDE: What did he ask you?

SARGENT: He said do you know, or can you tell me, of Menlove Gardens East? I said there is no Menlove Gardens East, there is a Menlove Gardens North, South and West. He said I have been to Menlove Gardens West number twenty five. The person I am looking for does not live there, and the numbers are all even and I suggested to him that he should try 25 Menlove Avenue. He said whereabouts is it? I said in the second or third block. He said thank you and turned as if to go away, and said do you know where I can see a directory? I said yes, you can see one down Allerton Road, or if you do not see one down there, you can see one down at the police station. Which I pointed out to him.

HEMMERDE: Or at the post office?

SARGENT: Or at the post office.

HEMMERDE: Had he said anything to you about who he was?

SARGENT: He said I am an insurance agent looking for a Mr Qualtrough who rang up the club and left a message for me with my colleague to visit Mr Qualtrough up at 25 Menlove Gardens East.

HEMMERDE: Was anything said about the time?

SARGENT: Yes. He then said it is not eight o'clock yet and pulled out his watch. I also did the same. He said it is just a quarter to. I glanced at my watch and saw it was a quarter to. He then left and walked across down Allerton Road. I did not see the accused afterwards.

This concludes Sargent's evidence which was not challenged by the defending counsel. Several matters are worthy of note at this point. Wallace had been positively informed by two people, Sydney Green (the fifth person Wallace spoke to in his search for Menlove Gardens East) and James Sargent, who knew the district well, the latter a police officer, that there was no such place as Menlove Gardens East. Yet he continued to make enquiries. Secondly, the message he had received from Beattie did not include a request by Qualtrough to phone him. Clearly this was so because he left an address but no telephone number. Thirdly, his stated unfamiliarity with Menlove Avenue was contrary to his experience as on a number of occasions he had passed through that road on his way to Calderstones Park with his wife Julia.

Wallace was directed at the post office to a newsagent's shop. Lily Pinches, the manageress of the shop in Allerton Road takes up the story at the trial:

PINCHES: I am the manageress of a newsagents shop 130 Allerton Road. On January 20th the accused came into my shop after eight o'clock in the evening. He asked for a directory.

COUNSEL [MR WALSH, Junior Counsel for the Prosectuion]: When he got it did he say anything?

PINCHES: No. Not until he had looked through it.

COUNSEL: What did he say then?

PINCHES: He asked me did I know what he was looking for, and I said No. He said 25 Menlove Gardens East.

COUNSEL: What did you say?

PINCHES: I said there was no 25 Menlove Gardens East, there was only South and West.

COUNSEL: Then, I understand, you looked up your account book?

PINCHES: Yes.

COUNSEL: And you found there was a 25 West?

PINCHES: No. They are not customers of our shop.

COUNSEL: Did the accused say anything then to you?

30

PINCHES: No.

COUNSEL: After you had said there was no 25 West in your account book, did he say anything? Did he say he had been there?

PINCHES: When I told him we had no 25 West, he said he had been there, and it was not the people he wanted.

Two points are mostly of note in Lily Pinches evidence. First it was put to her, clearly on instructions by Roland Oliver, that Wallace had mentioned to her the name of Qualtrough. This she firmly denied. Secondly she maintained that it was well after eight that Wallace had left the shop. Yet Wallace maintained that he had caught the 8.00pm tram home.

The question is a simple one. Was Wallace engaged on a genuine search, or was he setting up a skilful alibi for himself? Years later, the trial judge Mr Justice Wright, made this comment:

> Never forget that Wallace was a chess player ... I should say that, broadly speaking, any man with common sense would have said that Wallace's alibi was too good to be true, but that is not an argument you can hang a man on. So many strange things happen in life.

The jury in the Wallace trial have been criticised for the brief period of one hour it took them to reach their verdict. Particularly so since the Crown case rested entirely on circumstantial evidence. But let us remember this, a jury has one advantage over criminologists, writers and indeed the appeal court itself. The jury hears and sees the defendant, they and they alone are in a position to judge by his appearance and the way in which he or she gives their evidence, whether they believe or disbelieve what is said. They and they alone are best placed to distinguish between a poor, but honest, witness and a skilful liar. With this in mind let us see how Wallace responded to cross-examination on the matter of his search for Qualtrough.

HEMMERDE: I suppose the slightest enquiry at the Prudential Office would have told you the town of Liverpool is divided into blocks, each under an agent, and then there is a superintendent over the agent. It would have been the simplest thing in the world to find out through the machinery at the hands of the Prudential whether there was such a place?

WALLACE: It was not necessary.

HEMMERDE: Then when you went up to Penny Lane, you know now, at the terminus there. You were a very few yards away from Menlove Gardens East?

WALLACE: Yes.

HEMMERDE: Did it ever occur to you to ask the policeman there on point duty where it was?

WALLACE: No.

HEMMERDE: If you had you would have learned at once it was not there?

WALLACE: The tram conductor gave me sufficient evidence to show I had only to take the car on the right route and I would be where I wanted to be.

HEMMERDE: You were not asking the tram conductor where you were?

WALLACE: No. But he knew the route.

HEMMERDE: Would you describe yourself as a very talkative and communicative man? Rather the contrary are you not?

WALLACE: I do not know how I could describe myself. I leave others to do that.

HEMMERDE: Would you not say you are a person who would not talk more than is necessary?

WALLACE: I would not say.

HEMMERDE: Do you know the witness Phillips, the conductor, says three times you told him you wanted to go to Menlove Gardens East.

WALLACE: That may be so.

HEMMERDE: And once you told him you were a complete stranger in the district and had important business.

WALLACE: Yes.

HEMMERDE: Had you important business?

WALLACE: Yes, because it might have meant money to put into my pocket.

HEMMERDE: And you did not know who the person was?

WALLACE: No. I did not.

HEMMERDE: Do you know the next conductor, Thompson, says you asked him about Menlove Gardens East and you told him I am a complete stranger round here?

WALLACE: Yes.

HEMMERDE: And you know the police constable says that you asked him where Menlove Gardens East was?

WALLACE: Yes.

HEMMERDE: Had you already been told by the young clerk, Green, that there was no such place?

WALLACE: Yes.

HEMMERDE: And having been told by the police constable there was no such place, did you then go to the newsagent, Miss Pinches, and did you speak to her about looking for Menlove Gardens East?

WALLACE: Yes, I think so.

HEMMERDE: She says you did?

WALLACE: Yes.

HEMMERDE: And did you learn from her there was no such place?

WALLACE: I did.

HEMMERDE: As a matter of fact, does it not strike you, looking back upon it now, that all these enquiries were absolutely unnecessary. One simple enquiry of the policeman on point duty would have done it?

WALLACE: No, it does not strike me at all as being out of the way.

HEMMERDE: Where is Mr Crewe generally during the day?

WALLACE: At his office.

HEMMERDE: And that is on the telephone?

Walalce: The office is on the telephone.

HEMMERDE: You had only to ring up Mr Crewe and find out where Menlove Gardens East was, if it was near to him?

WALLACE: I could have done that but I did not think of it.

HEMMERDE: Then again, you say on the night at the café you were making so much of the name Qualtrough and talking to two of the members about it as a curious name?

WALLACE: No. I was talking to Mr Caird. It just occurred to me it was rather a curious name, and I simply asked Mr Caird had he heard of the name, and he had, but it was an entirely new name to me. It did not strike me there was anything unnatural in such a conversation.

HEMMERDE: Does not the whole thing strike you as very remarkable, that a man who does not know you should ring you up for business in another district, and expect you to go there and yet without knowing whether you had gone there or not, come and wait outside your house for the chance of murdering your wife?

WALLACE: Yes.

HEMMERDE: If you had been given a right address of course, you need not make a number of enquiries, one would have been sufficient, you follow what I mean?

WALLACE: Yes.

HEMMERDE: The wrong address is essential to the creation of evidence for the alibi. Do you follow that?

WALLACE: No I do not follow you.

HEMMERDE: If you had been told Menlove Gardens West, the first enquiry would have landed you there.

WALLACE: Yes.

HEMMERDE: If you are told of an address which does not exist, you can ask at seven or eight people. Every one of whom would be a witness where you were?

WALLACE: Yes

Wallace told the court that after leaving the newsagent he caught a tram home, having abandoned his quest. He said that by this time he was feeling 'uneasy'. At this point the evidence of Lily Hall becomes relevant. Lily Hall and her mother had frequently chatted with Julia Wallace after the service at Holy Trinity Church. She knew Wallace well by sight and had done for three or four years. She said that she had last seen Wallace on the day of the murder at 8.45pm near his house at the bottom of the entry to Richmond Park. He was talking to another man. Her evidence was strengthened by the fact that the police arranged an identity parade at which she picked out Wallace without hesitation. She proved a poor witness at the question of which direction she was taking when she made her observation and the man Wallace was allegedly speaking with was never traced. Nevertheless, it remains a fact that Lily Hall's knowledge of Wallace by sight was not challenged, nor was the evidence that she picked him out without hesitation at the identification parade. The significance of her evidence is that Wallace denied both the incident and any knowledge of Lily Hall. There was nothing to link the episode directly to the murder, but if Lily was right one wonders what was Wallace's motive for telling a lie. Secondly, Lily had the impression that Wallace, so far from hurrying home, was behaving normally as though there was no emergency.

It should also be noted that when, at the trial, the neighbour Mr Johnston was asked how Wallace was walking he replied 'In his ordinary way'. It has been suggested that Wallace may have had a confederate in the crime, but that would seem unlikely. A murderer would hardly want to be still hanging about in the neighbourhood at 8.40pm. Nor would he wish to dispose of blood-stained clothing and the murder instrument and then return to the scene afterwards.

So we come to Wallace's arrival at 29 Wolverton Street, and his horrific discovery.

CHAPTER FIVE

THE SCENE OF HORROR

Few more brutal murders can ever have been committed, this elderly lonely woman literally hacked to death for apparently no reason at all.

> Edward George Hemmerde opening the case for the crown in the trial of William Herbert Wallace for the murder of Julia Wallace.

There can be no doubt at all that this poor woman was done to death by, first a very crushing blow and then, if she was not already dead, by a succession of ten other blows.

> Mr Justice Wright, the judge at the trial of Wallace.

If as we have seen, the conduct of Wallace during his search for Menlove Gardens East gives rise to widely differing interpretations, the same can be said for his behaviour on reaching home and the discovery of his wife's bloody and battered body

Wallace arrived home at 8.45pm. He tried the front door, but by his own account given at the trial, could not turn the key at all. Consequently, he went to the rear of the premises. He entered the back yard by a door which had no lock, crossed the yard and tried the rear door of the house. Again, he failed to secure an entry. He returned to the front, but again had no success. Finally he went once more to the back entrance.

If opinions have differed about the correct inferences to be drawn from the behaviour of Wallace on the hunt for Menlove Gardens East, the same is true regarding his conduct on his arrival back at Wolverton Street. Supporters of the innocence of Wallace have always maintained that his words and actions were perfectly normal for a man who, although normally extremely self controlled, had undergone a most terrible shock. Those who assert his guilt contend that he was disguising his own dreadful crime behind a show of shock and dismay, put on for the benefit of the two witnesses who were with him at the time. Those witnesses were John Sharpe Johnston and his wife Florence Sarah Johnston, his next door neighbours at 31 Wolverton Street. John worked as an engineer in the shipyards of Cammel Laird on the Birkenhead side of the Mersey. John and Florence had been neighbours of the Wallace's for ten years, yet had only entered their home three times. However, they were on friendly terms with William and Julia. They gave evidence in the trial that had never seen or heard any quarrel between the Wallaces and to the best of their knowledge they were a devoted couple. Certainly the close proximity of the two houses and the fact of the thin walls would have made John and Florence well aware of any noisy disturbance next door. They heard none, although they did hear the musical duets which frequently occurred.

The Johnston's were going out that evening, and there can be little doubt that their meeting up with Wallace was by chance, and not by any design on his part as has been suggested. Mrs Johnston heard Wallace knocking at his back door. This was prior to his return to his front door to try once more which was also unsuccessful. The key would turn, but would not unlock the door. Wallace gave evidence in his trial that there had been trouble with the front door lock and Hemmerde, in his cross examination, questioned him at length on the subject of his difficulty in obtaining entry to his house. It seems to this author however that there is little in these matters to substantiate the charge of murder against Wallace.

There are though, two points of interest. The first is that Wallace affirmed that when he left the house by the back exit he invariably instructed his wife to bolt the door. He agreed that on this occasion he did not hear the bolt fall into place. One wonders why, if he was concerned about his wife's safety in his absence, as he said was the case, he did not ensure that this was done. The second is that, notwithstanding the claim by Wallace that he was 'uneasy' on his return, as one may well imagine, on his approach to his house he was described by the Johnston's as 'walking in the ordinary way'.

Now for an accurate picture of the scene at this crucial phase of the case, let us let us turn once more to the transcript of the evidence at the trial:

COUNSEL [MR WALSH]: You are an engineer, and you live at 358 Townend Avenue, Liverpool?

MR JOHNSTON: Yes.

COUNSEL: Did you move there in January last from 31 Wolverton Street?

MR JOHNSTON: Yes.

COUNSEL: You lived next door to the prisoner?

MR JOHNSTON: Yes.

COUNSEL: I understand you have not seen Mrs Wallace this year?

MR JOHNSTON: No.

COUNSEL: Do you remember the night she was murdered?

MR JOHNSTON: Yes.

COUNSEL: At about quarter to nine were you going out of your house?

36

MR JOHNSTON: Yes.

COUNSEL: Were you with your wife?

MR JOHNSTON: Yes.

COUNSEL: How do you know the time?

MR JOHNSTON: By the clock before I came out.

COUNSEL: When you are looking at your front door in Wolverton Street, Mr Wallace's door is on the left of your door?

MR JOHNSTON: Yes.

COUNSEL: So looking at the back door, his back door is on your right?

MR JOHNSTON: That is right.

COUNSEL: Which way out did you go that night?

MR JOHNSTON: The back way.

COUNSEL: Can you say whom you saw when you went out?

MR JOHNSTON: As I opened the door to let Mrs Johnston go out, Mr Wallace just passed.

COUNSEL: Had he come from the top of the entry, the top of the passage?

MR JOHNSTON: From the Breck Road end.

COUNSEL: Tell me exactly what you mean by passed. Was he hurrying, walking or running?

MR JOHNSTON: Walking in the ordinary way, towards his back door.

COUNSEL: Did your wife say anything to him?

MR JOHNSTON: My wife said 'Good evening Mr Wallace'.

COUNSEL: Did you think there was anything unusual from his manner?

MR JOHNSTON: He seemed anxious when he asked Mrs Johnston a question.

COUNSEL: When your wife had said 'Good evening Mr Wallace', what did he say?

MR JOHNSTON: Have you heard anything unusual tonight?

COUNSEL: Then what did your wife say?

MR JOHNSTON: She said 'No why? What has happened?'

COUNSEL: Did Mr Wallace say anything?

MR JOHNSTON: He said he had been round to the front door and also been to the back, and could not get in. The doors were fastened against him.

COUNSEL: What did you say to him then?

MR JOHNSTON: I suggested that he tried the door again, that is the back door, and if he could not open it, I would get my key out of my back door and try.

COUNSEL: Whereabouts were you when this conversation took place?

MR JOHNSTON: We were all standing in the entry, before the door into the entry had been opened.

COUNSEL: When you said try again and you would see, what did he do?

MR JOHNSTON: He went up to the door.

COUNSEL: Did Mr Wallace say anything when he went in, or when he went up the yard?

MR JOHNSTON: When he got to the door he called out it opens now.

COUNSEL: Were you able to hear, from where you were, whether he tried with his key or anything?

MR JOHNSTON: No. He did not seem to try the key, he seemed to turn the knob in the usual way.

COUNSEL: And said it opens now?

MR JOHNSTON: Yes.

MR JUSTICE WRIGHT: Could you see?

MR JOHNSTON: Yes. I could see him at the door my Lord.

COUNSEL: And it seemed to open quite easily?

MR JOHNSTON: Yes. There was no violence in the action of opening the door.

COUNSEL: Did you notice anything about the house while you were waiting outside?

MR JOHNSTON: Yes. The light in the middle bedroom was low and the small one in the back room.

MR JUSTICE WRIGHT: In the middle bedroom the windows look onto the yard, you would see them?

MR JOHNSTON: Yes. My Lord.

COUNSEL: Did you hear anything when Mr Wallace had gone in?

MR JOHNSTON: After he entered the house I heard him call out twice.

COUNSEL: Did you hear what it was?

MR JOHNSTON: No. I could not make out the name.

MR JUSTICE WRIGHT: He called out something?

MR JOHNSTON: Yes. A word.

COUNSEL: Did you notice anything else?

MR JOHNSTON: Yes. Just after he called out, the light was turned up in the middle bedroom.

MR JUSTICE WRIGHT: You could not say, I suppose, where he was when he called out?

MR JOHNSTON: I should say he was just at the top of the stairs, my Lord.

COUNSEL: Did you notice anything else after the light had been turned up?

MR JOHNSTON: Yes, a match I think had been struck in the small room, at the top of the stairs, which looks into the entry.

COUNSEL: What happened then?

MR JOHNSTON: Shortly after, Mr Wallace came into the yard.

COUNSEL: Can you say how long after, or give a rough idea?

MR JOHNSTON: Do you mean after the light was struck?

COUNSEL: Yes, after the light was struck.

MR JUSTICE WRIGHT: After the match was struck how long was it before Mr Wallace came out into the yard?

MR JOHNSTON: I would say a minute and a half at the most.

MR JUSTICE WRIGHT: A very short time?

COUNSEL: A minute and a half after, he came out?

MR JOHNSTON: Yes.

MR JUSTICE WRIGHT: Can you give any idea how long it was after he went into the house that he called out twice? Have you any idea about that?

MR JOHNSTON: It would take about the same time my Lord.

MR JUSTICE WRIGHT: Then I will say after about a minute and a half. It is only rough of course, a short time you mean?

MR JOHNSTON: Yes a short time.

COUNSEL: Did he run out or just walk out?

MR JOHNSTON: He hurried out.

COUNSEL: What did he say?

MR JOHNSTON: He said come and see, she has been killed.

COUNSEL: Are you sure that is what he said?

MR JOHNSTON: Yes.

COUNSEL: What was his manner when he said that?

MR JOHNSTON: He seemed a bit excited.

COUNSEL: When he said that did you go into the house?

MR JOHNSTON: Yes; we all went in.

Let us pause at this point. We now have the picture of Wallace on his return to his house. His sense of foreboding has been, according to him, greatly increased due to his difficulty in gaining access to his home. Then, which we have no option but to accept, he encounters by chance the two neighbours. It is interesting to contemplate what he would have done had they not been there. The criticism has been raised that he did not himself go to the police officer who would have been on duty nearby. There seems to be little substance in this point. After the discovery of his wife's body an innocent Wallace would clearly have been in a state of shock. Mr Johnston said he would go for the police and for medical assistance and there was no reason why Wallace should not have been content for him to do so.

What about the general manner of Wallace at the terrible scene? This has been the subject of much discussion and undoubtedly weighed heavily with the police and also, at the trial, with the jury. After his grim discovery

Wallace, came out of the house and said to the Johnstons 'Come and see she has been killed'. There was no crying out in an agony of distress, no instant floods of tears, no rushing outside. The inference is, of course, that having himself murdered his wife he knew perfectly well what he would find and therefore would suffer none of the shock endured by a blameless husband who has found the brutally murdered body of his beloved partner.

This aspect of the case must be borne in mind throughout, since it greatly influenced a number of witnesses and certainly had a bearing on the verdict of the jury. Yet, as in so much in this extraordinary case, there is a contrary inference which can be drawn. Had Wallace shown great emotion he might have been accused of putting on a convincing act to cover up his own guilt. Either way he was bound to attract suspicion.

Now let us consider the events inside the house after Wallace entered with the Johnstons:

COUNSEL: What did you see?

MR JOHNSTON: Mrs Wallace lying on the floor.

MR JUSTICE WRIGHT: You all went in, through the kitchen into the sitting room?

MR JOHNSTON: Yes, my Lord, right into the front room.

COUNSEL: Just say exactly what you saw.

MR JOHNSTON: As we went in, I saw the body lying diagonally across the room, the feet towards the fireplace and the head towards the door.

[Witness is shown photographs.]

COUNSEL: I want you to tell me, if you can, how far her head would be from the door?

MR JOHNSTON: The position of the head, when we were all in, I should say was eighteen inches from the edge of the door.

COUNSEL: Was there a light in the room?

MR JOHNSTON: Yes.

COUNSEL: Which one was it that was lit?

MR JOHNSTON: To the right hand of the fireplace.

COUNSEL: How near the body did you go?

MR JOHNSTON: Well I stooped down after I got into the room, and the wife also stooped down.

COUNSEL: What did you do when you stooped down?

MR JOHNSTON: I just looked over the body.

COUNSEL: Then what did your wife do? Did she do anything?

MR JOHNSTON: Yes. My wife held Mrs Wallace's hand.

COUNSEL: Which hand?

MR JOHNSTON: The left hand.

COUNSEL: You went out then, I understand, the three of you?

MR JOHNSTON: Yes we went out.

COUNSEL: Where did you go? Into the kitchen?

MR JOHNSTON: Into the kitchen.

COUNSEL: What did the accused say when you went into the kitchen?

MR JOHNSTON: He pointed to a lid on the floor, which he said belonged to a cabinet, which had been wrenched off.

COUNSEL: What did he say?

MR JOHNSTON: Then he reached up onto a shelf and took a cash box down.

COUNSEL: Is that the cash box there [produced]?

MR JOHNSTON: I only saw the lid.

COUNSEL: Is that the lid.

MR JOHNSTON: The lid was lying this way.

COUNSEL: He pointed this out and said that it had been wrenched off?

MR JOHNSTON: Yes.

COUNSEL: When he had taken down this cash box, what did he say?

MR JOHNSTON: I asked him if anything was missing.

COUNSEL: And then.

MR JOHNSTON: He replied about £4 but he could not say exactly until he had seen his books.

COUNSEL: Did you say anything else to him?

MR JOHNSTON: Yes, I said will you look upstairs and see if everything is alright before I go for the police and the doctor?

COUNSEL: Did he go upstairs?

MR JOHNSTON: Yes.

COUNSEL: How soon did he come down?

MR JOHNSTON: Up and down immediately: he did not stay any length of time at all.

COUNSEL: Then when he came down what did he say?

MR JOHNSTON: He said There is £5 in a jar they have not taken.

COUNSEL: Can you tell what his attitude, his demeanour, was during this time, after he had gone in from the yard into the front room and gone into the kitchen, and reached down this cash box?

MR JOHNSTON: He appeared to me as though he was suffering from a shock. He was quiet, walking round, he did not shout or anything like that.

When Johnston went for the police Wallace and Florence Johnston were left alone. Florence gave evidence at the trial similar to that of her husband prior to his departure. She described the finding of the body and the words of Wallace 'they have finished her, look at the brains' and her own comment while looking round the room 'whatever have they used?'. Then there entered into the mystery the presence of Wallace's mackintosh, crumpled up, and partially almost hidden under the body. Wallace came round the body and said 'whatever was she doing with her mackintosh and my mackintosh?' Wallace inspected the garment and admitted it was his.

They returned to the kitchen where Mrs Johnston, assisted by Wallace lit a fire. She was questioned at the trial about the attitude of Wallace at this time:

COUNSEL: Can you tell me what his attitude was the whole of this time? Did he seem excited or did he seem calm, collected or what?

MRS JOHNSTON: At first he was quite collected.

COUNSEL: What do you mean by at first?

MRS JOHNSTON: Before my husband left for the police.

COUNSEL: He was quite collected?

MRS JOHNSTON: Yes.

COUNSEL: And then?

MRS JOHNSTON: Then twice he showed emotion by putting his head in his hands, and he sobbed.

COUNSEL: Where were you when he did that?

MRS JOHNSTON: In the kitchen.

COUNSEL: Was there anybody else in?

MRS JOHNSTON: No.

COUNSEL: How long would it be that he was showing his emotion by sobbing?

MRS JOHNSTON: Just momentarily.

COUNSEL: Apart from that what was he like?

MRS JOHNSTON: He was mostly collected.

CHAPTER SIX

THE POLICE IN ACTION

The Liverpool City Police Force in 1931 has been subjected to a great deal of Criticism. How justified is this?

The police strike of 1919 was set off by the Police Bill which formed the Police Federation and was considered by officers to reduce the power of their union. The places chiefly affected were Liverpool and London. It resulted in many officers being dismissed, after which a large number of volunteers took their place. This may well have caused a reduction in efficiency, but it is surely an exaggeration to say, as Jonathan Goodman does in his very thorough study of the Wallace case *The Killing of Julia Wallace*:

> By 1931 much of the Liverpool City Police Force was hardly up to the task of dealing with parking offences, let alone a full scale murder investigation.

It should be borne in mind that investigation techniques, such as for example finger printing, were far less developed than is the case today. Communications were more limited and forensic science generally not so advanced. Above all, DNA, which can identify a guilty criminal by the analysis of body fluids such as blood, saliva and semen, was as yet undiscovered. The police did not have the benefit of the Crown Prosecution Service to advise them on the prospects of conviction in pending criminal charges, and in the less serious cases in magistrates' courts police officers themselves presented their cases instead of being represented by solicitors or counsel. Certainly, things had improved since the time when Jack the Ripper was hunted through the London fog by a pack of bloodhounds, but police methods of enquiry had far to go.

The first police officer to arrive on the scene was police constable Frederick Robert Williams. PC Williams had been on duty in Anfield Road near Wallace's house. He was admitted by Wallace with the words 'something terrible has happened officer'. Williams was asked at the trial what he saw when he enter the sitting room. He replied:

> In the sitting room, on the mat in front of the fireplace, I saw the body of a woman, who I knew to be Mrs Julia Wallace; her head was towards the sitting room, and her feet were towards the right hand side of the fireplace. She was lying in a twisted position. I felt her right wrist and could feel no pulsation.

Williams said that her flesh was still slightly warm. Wallace then made a statement to the officer; after saying that he did not know how it had happened, Wallace continued:

> At 6.45 I left the house in order to go to Menlove Gardens and my wife accompanied me to the back yard door. She walked a little way down the entry with me, and she returned and bolted the back yard door. She would then be alone in the house. I went to Menlove Gardens, to find that the address which had been given me was wrong. Becoming suspicious, I returned home and went to the front door. I inserted my key in the front door, to find I could not open it. I went round to the back, round to the back entry door; it was closed but not bolted. I went up the yard and tried the back kitchen door, but it would not open. I again went to the front door, and this time found the door was bolted. I hurried round to the back and up the back yard, and tried the back kitchen door, and this time found it would open. I entered the house and this is what I found.

This statement of Wallace's is important. This is so, first because what a suspect says when first questioned is revealing because he or she has not had time to invent a story which may not be true. Secondly, it must be said in fairness to Wallace that his original statement was entirely consistent with the account he gave on later occasions to the police and at his trial. The discrepancies, although emphasised by Edward Hemmerde at the trial, are not of great significance.

PC Williams then made a search of the house – the first police officer to do so. He was taken through this at the trial by Hemmerde:

HEMMERDE: Did you then proceed, accompanied by the accused, to search and examine the house?

WILLIAMS: Yes.

HEMMERDE: What did you find in the middle bedroom?

WILLIAMS: In the middle bedroom the gas jet was lit. I asked the accused if this light was burning when he entered the house. He replied I changed myself in this room before leaving.

HEMMERDE: Did you notice anything on the mantelpiece.

WILLIAMS: On the mantelpiece I noticed an ornament from which five or six £1 pound notes were protruding.

Henmmerde: Meanwhile what did the accused do?

WILLIAMS: The accused took hold of the ornament and partly extracted the notes, and said Here is some money which has not been touched.

HEMMERDE: What did you do?

WILLIAMS: I requested the accused to replace the ornament and the notes in their original positions, and this he did.

44

HEMMERDE: What did you do next?

WILLIAMS: To the right of the fireplace I noticed a curtained recess. I approached this and the accused said: My wife's clothes are out there, they have not been touched.

HEMMERDE: Did you look in the recess?

WILLIAMS: I looked in the recess and apparently they were undisturbed, they were alright.

HEMMERDE: When you looked in that recess, did the accused say anything?

WILLIAMS: The accused said There appears to have been no one here.

HEMMERDE: Then, I think, there is a back room which has been converted into a laboratory?

WILLIAMS: Yes.

HEMMERDE: Did the accused say anything there?

WILLIAMS: He said Everything seems to be alright here.

HEMMERDE: Did you then go into the bathroom?

WILLIAMS: Yes.

HEMMERDE: Was there any light in there?

WILLIAMS: There was a small light there.

HEMMERDE: Did you say anything to the accused?

WILLIAMS: I am not quite sure whether I said was this light burning when you entered the house? or Is this light usually kept on?

HEMMERDE: What did he say?

WILLIAMS: He replied; we usually have a light here.

HEMMERDE: Did you then go into the front bedroom?

WILLIAMS: Yes.

HEMMERDE: Was there a light in there?

WILLIAMS: No.

HEMMERDE: What condition was it in?

WILLIAMS: The room was in a state of disorder, the bedclothes were half on the bed and half on the floor; there were a couple of pillows lying near the fireplace; there was a dressing table in the room, containing drawers and a mirror and also a wardrobe; the drawers of the dressing table were shut and the doors of the wardrobe were shut.

HEMMERDE: Nothing was open on the dressing table or in the wardrobe?

WILLIAMS: Nothing whatever.

HEMMERDE: Where did you go then?

WILLIAMS: We returned downstairs to the kitchen.

HEMMERDE: When in the kitchen did you notice anything?

WILLIAMS: I noticed the door of a small cabinet had been broken in two pieces.

HEMMERDE: Is that the cabinet and the broken doors? [Exhibited]

WILLIAMS: Yes, that is the cabinet, and that is the broken piece of the door.

HEMMERDE: Did the accused point anything out to you?

WILLIAMS: The accused pointed out to me a small cash box which was lying on top of the bookcase to the left of the fireplace.

HEMMERDE: Did he say anything about it?

WILLIAMS: He said there was about £4 altogether and it was gone.

HEMMERDE: Did he pick up anything else and show it to you?

WILLIAMS: The accused picked up a ladies handbag, which was lying on the chair near the table.

HEMMERDE: Did he do anything with this bag?

WILLIAMS: The accused opened the bag and took out a £1 note and some silver. He did say something which I cannot remember, referring to his wife's money.

HEMMERDE: When you entered the sitting room, as you were looking round, what did the accussed do?

WILLIAMS: The accused stepped round the body near the side-board, and lit the left hand gas mantle.

HEMMERDE: Did you then leave the room?

WILLIAMS: We did. I closed the room door behind me.

HEMMERDE: Up to that time when you have just told my Lord and the jury that he lighted the other light, what had been the demeanour of the accused?

WILLIAMS: He was cool and calm, well, I thought he was extraordinarily cool and calm.

HEMMERDE: After that you went into the kitchen I think?

WILLIAMS: Yes. We returned to the kitchen.

HEMMERDE: Did you say anything to him there?

WILLIAMS: I noticed the window of the kitchen was covered with heavy curtains, these I slightly parted. I said to the accused, did you notice any lights in the house when you entered? He said with the exception of the lights upstairs, the house was in darkness I then asked him, when he first entered the yard did he notice any light escaping through the curtains and he replied that the curtains would not allow the light to escape.

HEMMERDE: Did you ask him, or did he say whether or not when he went into the kitchen there was any light there?

WILLIAMS: He did tell me that there was no light in the kitchen.

HEMMERDE: When he entered?

WILLIAMS: Yes, when he entered.

HEMMERDE: And it was after he said that, that you asked him about whether he had noticed anything when he came up the yard?

WILLIAMS: Yes.

HEMMERDE: A little time later, did you again enter the sitting room?

WILLIAMS: I did.

HEMMERDE: And at that time had police sergeant Breslin arrived?

WILLIAMS: He had.

HEMMERDE: When you went into the sitting room, did you say anything to the accused?

WILLIAMS: I spoke to both the accused and police sergeant Breslin, and said that looks like a mackintosh.

HEMMERDE: Where were you when you said that looks like a mackintosh?

WILLIAMS: I was inside the living room.

HEMMERDE: Were you standing up or sitting down?

WILLIAMS: Standing up.

HEMMERDE: When you said that looks like a mackintosh what did the accused say?

WILLIAMS: The accused was standing in the doorway. He looked into the hall, at the same time saying it is an old one of mine.

This is an appropriate point at which to pause and consider two matters which are both of considerable importance in the case and both add to its mystery. These are, first the mackintosh and secondly the condition of the house, in particular the shambolic state of the upstairs front bedroom. Normally in a murder investigation, those items which are considered by the police to be useful clues in finding the culprit either point to the guilt of the accused person or turn out to have no significance and therefore count towards his innocence. In the instance of the mackintosh, there is further mystery which carries the case no further for or against Wallace.

As we have seen, Wallace himself commented upon the fact that an old mackintosh, belonging to himself, was folded around the right shoulder of the body of Julia. He said to PC Williams 'it is an old one of mine'.

Superintendent Moore, who was in charge of the enquiry, arrived at 29 Wolverton Street at 10.05pm on 20 January, the night of the murder. He dealt with the matter of the mackintosh in his evidence in court:

HEMMERDE: And you then went back into the sitting-room?

MOORE: Yes. I got down and carefully examined the mackintosh, which was placed on the deceased's right side.

HEMMERDE: Can you tell my Lord and the jury, was there any part of the body resting on it?

MOORE: No part of the body was resting on it.

HEMMERDE: You saw it there?

MOORE: It was like this, as though it had been put in this position round the shoulder and tucked in by the side, as though the body was a living person and you were trying to make it comfortable. No portion was resting under the body, I called the accused in from the kitchen, and I was standing inside the doorway. He came and stood on my left, slightly behind me. I said to him is this your mackintosh? He stooped slightly and put his left hand to his chin. I looked at him, and he made no reply for perhaps half a minute or so. I said had Mrs Wallace a mackintosh like this? He remained in the same position and did not answer. The witness Sergeant Bailey was standing in front of me, by the sideboard, and I said take it up and let us have a look at it. I got hold of the sleeves and pulled it out like this and said it is a gent's mackintosh. By that time the accused had actually got hold of the mackintosh and was examining it.

HEMMERDE: Did he say anything?

MOORE: If there are two patches on the inside it is mine. By that time we found the two patches and almost in a continuing sentence he said it is mine .

HEMMERDE: Then did he say anything else?

MOORE: I wore it this morning, but the day turned out to be fine, I wore my fawn coat this afternoon. Of course it was not burnt like that when I wore it. I asked him where he had left it, he said hanging in the hall at half past one.

The case for the prosecution regarding the mackintosh was this: When Wallace bludgeoned his wife to death he wore the mackintosh in order to protect himself from the inevitable splashes of blood. Having done so he attempted to burn the incriminating garment. This he failed to do, and because it would be unthinkable to carry something covered with blood out of the house he was obliged to leave it with her body.

Edward Hemmerde, counsel for the Crown, dealt at some length with this aspect of the case in his opening speech to the jury, and then introduced a somewhat startling theory to remove the Crown's principal difficulty in their proceedings against Wallace: The failure of the police to find any trace of blood on the clothing or shoes of Wallace. Having conceded that Wallace admitted that the coat was his Hemmerde then continues:

That mackintosh was there, covered with blood, it was also badly burnt: a lot of it, quite a large part of it, as you will see was burnt. How does it come that that mackintosh was there, and that it was burnt? Had it taken fire by accident? If so, what from? Had it been burned by someone on purpose? And if so, who had burned it? This mackintosh was hanging up in the passage, he had worn it that day. It is found there, against the body with much blood upon it and apparently rolled up and pressed against the body after some attempt had been made, if it was not an accident, to burn it.

Just consider at this moment who had an interest in destroying that mackintosh? Assuming that someone had broken into that house – there is no trace at all that anyone did, but assuming that they did, and then killed this woman, it is possible that such a person might have taken down the raincoat, and put it on to prevent the blood getting upon his clothes – perfectly possible, but having done so, why should a stranger to her want to destroy the mackintosh? Having done this foul deed, what concern would it be for a man of criminal intention, who had come in there and killed this woman, to destroy someone else's raincoat? You will see it, you will form you own views as to how that came to be partly burnt, and you will have your own views, no doubt, as to what conclusion the condition of that leads you to. That is the position so far as that coat is concerned.

It was then that Hemmerde sprang his surprise.

I draw your attention to the fact that there is no blood whatsoever anywhere on the stairs, because the crown suggests to you that in this case whoever did this deed was taking elaborate precautions. The history of our own criminal courts shows what elaborate precautions people can sometimes take. One of the most famous criminal trials was of a man who committed a crime when he was naked. A man might perfectly well commit a crime wearing a raincoat, as one might wearing a dressing gown, and come down, when he is just going to do this, with nothing on onto which blood could fasten, and with anything like care, he might get away, leaving the raincoat there and go and perform the necessary washing if he was very careful. There was hot and cold water in the kitchen - running water. Whoever did this did not take advantage of that fact, but went upstairs, and, as I suggest to you, went upstairs with great caution.

In putting before the jury this possible scenario Hemmerde was on sensitive ground. He was entitled, within the rules which govern advocacy, to present a possible explanation for what would otherwise remain a mystery, but there have to be limits to this tactic. The function of an advocate is to argue the case on the basis of such facts as are before the court, not to toy with mere probabilities. This is particularly so in a criminal trial where the jury must be certain about the events on which they must reach a verdict. However, it may be legitimate to invite the persons of the jury to consider what was the likely course of events, providing it is made clear by counsel that what is being proposed is only a credible theory and no more. It is the responsibility of the judge to indicate in his or her summing-up how much weight should be placed upon it.

The defence, for their part, adopted a similar strategy in order to explain the burning of the raincoat. It was important to the case for Wallace to counter the damaging suggestion that he, and he alone, had the interest and the incentive to destroy the garment. This issue arose during the evidence of

Professor John MacFall, whose testimony on the medical aspects of the case we shall consider shortly:

HEMMERDE: Supposing someone had been wearing that? [the mackintosh]

MACFALL: That is the source of the blood from the front, and if anybody was wearing this then there had been a spurt of blood from the front, because it comes in this direction.

HEMMERDE: Looking at that, the suggestion has been made that the deceased might have thrown it over her shoulders to go to the door, and then to have been, I suppose struck when she had it on

MACFALL: When I saw it there was no suggestion from the appearance that that was the case

MR JUSTICE WRIGHT: You mean from the position?

MACFALL: Yes, it was tucked under the right shoulder almost in this direction [illustrating]. There was no suggestion of it having been on the arms whatever, nothing whatever.

Roland Oliver KC, defending, was anxious to press his own alternative proposition – that Julia Wallace goes to answer the door wearing the mackintosh around her shoulders because she had a cold and the weather was bitter in January. She admitted the murderer and, so the defence suggested, was lighting the gas fire when she was struck down. The burning occurred when the mackintosh touched the fire and this led to the burnt condition of Julia's skirt.

OLIVER: If she had that coat around her, and the gas fire was alight, and she fell when she was struck, so as to burn her skirt in the lit fire, do you not think it quite possible that that mackintosh swung round on to the fireplace and caught fire?

MACFALL: No, because there is no evidence of it having been on her right or left arm

OLIVER: Suppose it was around her shoulders and she collapsed, do you not see the possibility of the bottom of the mackintosh falling into the fire and getting burnt too?

MACFALL: There is the possibility.

It would have been difficult for MacFall to deny a possibility, and Oliver was within the ethics of advocacy in putting it to the witness. However, Oliver knew he was taking a chance, as he had earlier when he put it to Beattie that the voice of Qualtrough was nothing like the voice of Wallace. He might have got the wrong answer, something which a good advocate dreads.

In fact a photograph of the murder scene taken with the head near the camera shows that the gas fire was of the old variety recessed behind a grate. That would seem to make Oliver's theory unlikely. Like much else in this perplexing case the scorched mackintosh and skirt are a mystery. But on balance it would seem to be prejudicial to Wallace, rather than in his favour. Having worn the garment to commit the murder he would be faced with a dilemma. He could hardly leave the house carrying a blood soaked mackintosh. Therefore to burn it was the only option. Another killer would simply have left it as it was – content that it would bring suspicion to Wallace.

Now let us turn to the medical evidence in the case. Medical witnesses, that is to say those persons who are entitled by virtue of their qualifications to give expert evidence as to the time of death, the cause of death, and, as far as possible, indications of whom the guilty person may be, are distinct in one respect from all other people giving testimony in court. They are entitled, under the rules of evidence, to express an opinion. Every other witness may only speak as to his or her knowledge as a result of what they have seen, heard or personally experienced. They are not entitled to pronounce on any conclusion which they have drawn. The interpretation of evidence is for the jury. Medical evidence is the exception to this rule. Thus it is perfectly proper for counsel to ask a doctor or scientific expert: 'What did you deduce as the result of your examination?'

Expert witnesses, if they are very highly qualified and command a considerable reputation in their particular field are treated with great respect, because the assumption of the court is that not only are they exceptionally knowledgeable, but also their impartiality can be relied on. Their sole reason for appearing in the case is to contribute to the cause of justice by putting their talent at the service of the search for truth.

However, there is a danger inherent in this. If the expert is especially outstanding a weight may be given to his evidence solely on the basis of his reputation. The great forensic expert Bernard Spilsbury, at the height of his career, enjoyed an eminence close to infallibility. There may have been a good reason for this, but in his later days he made some serious mistakes. These, in the days of capital punishment, could be disastrous errors. Consequently, where medical issues are at stake it is common for the defence to call witnesses, who are also well qualified people, to contradict statements made by those summoned by the prosecution.

The primary medical witness called by the Crown in the Wallace case was Professor John Edward Wheatly MacFall. Professor MacFall who has been the subject of much discussion and some controversy amid criminologists and students of the case, was a colourful and what is sometimes termed 'larger than life character'. That he was highly qualified there is no disputing.

He was Professor of Forensic Medicine at the University of Liverpool and Examiner in Medical Jurisprudence at the Universities of Glasgow, Edinburgh, Manchester and Birmingham. In his younger days he had been an all-round athlete and held the combined universities record for putting the shot. While an officer in the Royal Army Medical Corps he was wounded twice and gassed. On the minus side he was known to be an opium smoker and was subject to personal criticism for being bombastic, and sometimes less than meticulous in his work.

Whether he deserved such severe strictures as those passed upon him by Jonathan Goodman in his book *The Killing of Julia Wallace* (Charles Scribner's Sons, 1969) is questionable. Goodman writes:

> Always an egotist, it would seem that the sudden and unnatural death of his younger son (who suffocated in his pillow at the age of fifteen) tilted Mac-Fall's mind towards megalomania. He deluded himself and, unfortunately a great many other people – with the idea that he was a sort of real life Dr Thorndike, He stated his opinions, often based on scanty evidence as facts; he refused to accept the arguments of others.

MacFall described in court what he saw when he arrived at 29 Wolverton Street:

> I saw the dead body of a woman lying on the hearth rug, face downwards and the face was turned to the left. The left arm was extended and the right arm was by the side of the body. The body was fully clothed and lay diagonally across the hearth rug. The head was by the corner of the rug nearest to the door. The head was badly battered on the left side above and in front of the ear, where there was a large open wound approximately half an inch by three inches, from which bone and brain substance were protruding. At the back and on the left side of the head, there was a great depression of the skull, with severe wounds. The hands were quite cold, the lower arms were cold, but the upper arms and the body were warm. Rigor mortis, the stiffening that follows death, was present in the upper part of the left arm and the neck. The head was turned to the left, and fixed by post mortem rigidity of the neck by about one o'clock, that is approximately two hours afterwards.

HEMMERDE: Three hours after?

MACFALL: Yes, three hours afterwards, that was practically when I was leaving, and I was watching the body in between and watching the process of this stiffening, it was about this time, about one o'clock, the post mortem rigidity had extended to the right arm and the right leg, but on my first observation, when I noted that the neck was stiff and the upper part of the left arm. My opinion was that death had taken place quite four hours before ten o'clock. On further examination of the body there was a little blood – staining of the hands. There was nothing clenched in the hands and nothing beneath the finger-nails

HEMMERDE: Before you go on; you say you formed the view of four hours. Could you give a definite minimum that it must have been, a certain time?

MACFALL: There is always a certain amount of possibility one way or the other, but the opinion I formed then was, that it was over four hours since this woman had been dead.

MR JUSTICE WRIGHT: That is at ten o'clock at night?

MACFALL: That would bring it back from ten o'clock to six o'clock.

HEMMERDE: What would you regard as the possible margin of error in that calculation?

MACFALL: It could not possibly be in this case more than an hour.

MR JUSTICE WRIGHT: One hour's error would bring it to seven o'clock; half an hour error would bring it to half past six?

MACFALL: Yes. But there is the other way, and I formed the opinion that it was four hours or more.

Now let us consider the following matters: First, the importance of the time at which the fatal blows were struck and its relevance to the guilt or innocence of Wallace; secondly, the tests applied by MacFall to ascertain this, and thirdly, the evidence of the other experts called compared with that of MacFall.

Experts, although impartial, are called as witnesses in the hope that what they have to say, will assist the case of the side that calls them, be it the Crown or the defence. Professor MacFall was a prosecution witness because those representing the Crown believed from statements he had already provided to them, that what he would say in court would strengthen the prosecution case. The question of the time of the attack which slew Julia was vitally important since it bore upon her husband's presence in, or absence from, the house when it took place.

There was no dispute that Wallace had been going about his normal work as an insurance agent, both in the morning and afternoon of 20 January. Wallace's own account of this was accepted by the court, and supported by witnesses on whom he called in connection with their various policies and payments. But thereafter what he told the police, and subsequently the court, was his own uncorroborated testimony. This was as follows: He ceased his work at about a few minutes to six, and that he got home shortly after six, he was at home with his wife until a quarter to seven when he left the house and proceeded to catch a tram at 7.06pm, to begin his journey in search of the mythical Menlove Gardens East.

The nub of the defence was that if Wallace left home at 6.45pm and Julia was seen alive at 6.30pm Wallace had very little time in which to commit the murder and also create the signs of an aborted burglary. Professor MacFall stuck to his opinion that death occurred at 6pm, but fortunately for Wallace, the milk boy insisted that Julia spoke to him at 6.30pm. But was Wallace truthful about 6.45pm being the time when he left the house? And, if he did in fact murder his wife, is it possible that he created the signs of disturbance at the house before and not after the killing? Certainly the evidence of the milk boy, Alan Close, cuts down the time available to Wallace very drastically, if it is to be argued that he was his wife's killer.

Furthermore, what undermines the evidence of Professor MacFall on the question of time and makes the task of the prosecution more difficult is the testimony of Wildman and Metcalf who were called by the defence. Alison Wildman, a girl of 16, was delivering newspapers in Wolverton Street. She had begun her round at 6.20pm, she told the court:

> I passed Holy Trinity Church clock at twenty five to seven and it takes me two minutes to walk to Wolverton Street so it would be twenty three minutes to seven when I got there

OLIVER: When you went away where was the boy [Close]?

WILDMAN: Still standing on the step

Douglas Metcalfe, another paper boy gave even more damaging evidence to the Crown case:

OLIVER: Do you remember the night of Mrs Wallace's death?

METCALFE: Yes.

OLIVER: Were you anywhere near Wolverton Street that evening?

METCALFE: Yes.

OLIVER: What time?

METCALFE: About twenty or a quarter to seven.

OLIVER: Why do you say that? How do you know the time?

METCALFE: I had to get to the Parochial hall to deliver a paper to Mrs Davies, and I asked one of the men what time it was, as I wanted to go to a match, and one man told me twenty to seven. Then I went to Campbell's and stood talking to some boys outside.

OLIVER: This is Campbell's Dancing Hall?

METCALFE: Yes; and I went back to some boys and stood talking about five minutes.

OLIVER: Who did you see?

METCALFE: I saw Wildman going down an entry leading off Wolverton Street.

OLIVER: You saw Wildman leaving Wolverton Street?

METCALFE: Yes.

OLIVER: Were you in this group on the evening of the 21st, the day after the murder, with Elsie Wright and the others?

METCALFE: Yes.

OLIVER: Did you hear Alan Close say what time it was that he had seen Mrs Wallace alive?

METCALFE: Yes; he said it was a quarter to seven.

OLIVER: Have you any doubt about that?

METCALFE: No sir.

A further witness to the same effect was Kenneth Campbell Caird:

OLIVER: Did you on the evening of the 21st January last, hear Alan Close say what time he last saw Mrs Wallace alive?

CAIRD: Yes; he said a quarter to seven.

Finally David Jones testified that he had delivered the Liverpool Echo every evening for four of five years at 29 Wolverton Street. He stated that on the evening of the murder he delivered the paper at 6.35pm, and that he saw nobody at the house.

Allowing for possible discrepancies, the upshot of these witnesses is that Julia Wallace was seen alive by Close after 6.30pm. If Wallace was correct that he left the house at 6.45 that leaves only around a quarter of an hour for the murder of Julia and the attendant activities of washing blood off himself and preparing the bogus signs of a burglary. Wallace then walked to the tram stop at the junction of West Derby Road and Belmont Road, caught a tram and boarded a second one in Smithdown Road, at 7.06pm. Various tests were applied by the police with which I will not weary the reader. Hemmerde failed to shake any of the young witnesses' evidence. If Wallace was guilty he worked with amazing speed.

Notwithstanding these difficulties MacFall flatly refused to change his estimate of the time of death as 6pm. Something that should not be overlooked at this crucial stage of the case are the statements of Walter Holme and his wife Bertha. On the evening of 20 January they were having tea in the kitchen of their home, 27 Wolverton Street next door to the Wallace's. At 6.30pm Mrs Holme heard the sound of knocking, and the sound of what she thought was someone falling. She asked her husband 'is that someone at our front door?' He said 'No. it's at the Wallace's'. At 6.35pm the Wallace's front door was heard to close. Were these sounds caused by Alan Close at number 29?

MacFall, who spent three hours with the body of Julia, described how she could have been sitting in a chair when the first ferocious blow was delivered. He also described the ten blows delivered to the head of the victim when she was on the floor. MacFall referred to the fact that there were blood splashes on the furniture and the walls, but that there were no other marks of blood elsewhere in the house except for a tiny spot on the toilet bowl upstairs. He agreed with Oliver that there was one dry towel in the bathroom and no signs of anyone having had a bath.

The controversial part of MacFall's evidence came when he dealt with Wallace's mental state:

HEMMERDE: Can you tell my Lord and the jury what was the demeanour of the accused when he was there?

MACFALL: I was very struck with it; it was abnormal.

HEMMERDE: In what way?

MACFALL: He was too quiet, too collected for a person whose wife has been killed in that way that he described. He was not nearly so affected as I was myself.

HEMMERDE: Do you happen to remember anything particular that led you to that conclusion?

MACFALL: I think he was smoking cigarettes most of the time. Whilst I was in the room examining the body and the blood, he came in smoking a cigarette, and he leant over on front of the sideboard and flicked the ash into a bowl upon the sideboard. It struck me at the time as being unnatural.

HEMMERDE: To do that would he have to lean across anything?

MACFALL: He did not come forward. I can recall his position at the moment; he leant forward so as not to step on the clot [a sketch made by the witness of the position of the injuries on the head of the victim is put in].

ROLAND OLIVER [cross examining]: I do not want to stop anything, but how can that indicate who did it?

MACFALL: I have a great reason for this myself.

HEMMERDE: Can you give, quite shortly, what your reason is?

MACFALL: I can. I formed an idea of the mental condition of the person who committed this crime. I have seen crimes, many of them of this kind, and know what the mental condition is. I know it was not an ordinary case of assault or serious injury. It was a case of frenzy.

That word 'frenzy' shook the court and had, we may assume a significant effect upon the jury. It also cast a new and influential light upon the whole case, particularly since the witness who used the word was so experienced a forensic expert as Professor MacFall. It suggested that the emotional element was paramount in the killing. There was a personal aspect to the murder which was completely incompatible with the defence theory that the primary motive of the guilty party was theft. Why on earth should an interloper, who had succeeded in talking Mrs Wallace into inviting him into the house, against her husband's advice, turn on her with such savagery? There were no signs of a struggle, no sign that she was slain while attempting to prevent him stealing anything in the house. Given that scenario the disproportion as between the motive and the assault is extraordinary.

The Judge made a modifying comment:

We may have already formed that opinion where blows are struck by anyone, that probably does produce frenzy, but that is a matter for the jury.

Roland Oliver in cross-examination tried not surprisingly, to undo the harm which had been done to his client's case:

OLIVER: With reference to the last matter, you have noticed that my client has been under medical observation as to his medical condition ever since his arrest?

MACFALL: I knew that he will have been.

OLIVER: If there is anything to be said about his medical condition, there are people who are competent to say it, who have lived with him.

MACFALL: Yes. I do not wish to express any opinion.

OLIVER: If this is the work of a maniac, and he is a sane man, he did not do it. Is that right?

MACFALL: He may be sane now.

OLIVER: If he has been sane all his life, and is sane now, it would be some momentary frenzy?

MACFALL: The mind is very peculiar.

OLIVER: It is a rash suggestion is it not?

MACFALL: Not the slightest. I have seen this sort of thing before, exactly the same thing.

OLIVER: Rash to suggest in a murder case. I suggest to you.

MACFALL: I do not suggest who did it at all.

OLIVER: The fact that a man has been sane for fifty two years, and has been sane while in custody for the last three months, would rather tend to prove that he has always been sane, would it not?

MACFALL: Not, necessarily.

OLIVER: Not necessarily?

MACFALL: No. We know very little about the private lives of people or their thoughts.

OLIVER: Let us go back. You have told the jury that you were very much struck with his demeanour. You noticed it at the time, and were very much struck with his callous demeanour?

MACFALL: I was.

OLIVER: Why did you not say so at the Police Court?

MacFall: I was not asked.

Oliver was on weak ground and he knew it. Murder is committed for a variety of motives: Passion, revenge, jealousy, gain and so on. Not all its perpetrators are insane. Some, like Heath and Haigh, and most serial killers, are clearly mentally deranged. But no one suggested that Crippin or Seddon were mad. As MacFall pointed out, the human mind is very peculiar. An apparently well behaved and perfectly normal person can explode into a fury or be driven to an extremity under the most intense pressure. He simply 'snaps'.

Oliver questioned MacFall on such matters as the precise position of Julia when she was hacked down, the inevitability of the murderer being splashed with blood on his face, hands and the lower part of his legs, notwithstanding the fact that he may have been wearing the mackintosh at the time; the fact that there were no signs in the bathroom of anyone having taken a bath; the small clot of blood on the toilet basin, which MacFall agreed might have been dropped by the police during their investigations, and finally the accuracy of the test he applied in order to ascertain the time of death. This last matter was important to the defence in order to undermine the Crown case that Wallace was in the house when Julia died.

MacFall was criticised, unsurprisingly, for the fact that he made no notes during his examination of the body. He was further censured for applying the notoriously unreliable rigor mortis test instead of taking the rectal temperature which is considered less likely to err.

Oliver: When did you first think the time of death is important?

MacFall: Immediately I examined the body.

Oliver: And you proceeded to ascertain, by a series of observations, first as to rigor mortis, and secondly as to the condition of the exuded blood?

MacFall: The blood is a help, but not so definite as rigor mortis.

Oliver: You put rigor mortis first, but the other did assist you to form your opinion?

MacFall: It did.

Oliver: How many notes did you make with regard to rigor mortis?

MacFall: None, I think.

Oliver: Can you show me one?

MacFall: I do not think I can.

Oliver: It comes to this does it not, that you, being intent from the start on the importance of rigor mortis as to the time of death, have not made one note with regard to rigor mortis?

MacFall: That is so.

OLIVER: Let us take the question of rigor. Rigor is a very fallible test as to the time of death?

MACFALL: Not in the present case of an ordinary person dying in health.

OLIVER: It is a very fallible factor, even in healthy people?

MACFALL: It is, just a little.

OLIVER: Does it depend, among other things, upon the muscularity of the person?

MACFALL: It does.

OLIVER: And the powerful and muscular body will be affected by rigor much more slowly?

MACFALL: Yes.

OLIVER: Than a feeble and frail lady?

MACFALL: Yes. She was not exactly frail; she was a feeble woman.

OLIVER: You have used the word frail.

MACFALL: Yes. She was a weak woman.

Oiver: Frail?

MACFALL: Yes. Frail.

OLIVER: Bearing in mind that this feeble and frail woman would more likely to be affected by rigor, are you going to swear she was killed more than three hours before you saw her?

MACFALL: No. I am not going to swear; I am going to give an opinion and I swear that the opinion that I shall give shall be an honest one.

MR JUSTICE WRIGHT: Then what is your opinion?

MACFALL: My opinion was formed at the time that the woman had been dead about four hours.

OLIVER: You saw her at 10.10pm?

MACFALL: Yes.

OLIVER: So if she was alive at half past six, your opinion is wrong?

MACFALL: Yes.

OLIVER: Does that not convince you what a fallible test rigor mortis is?

MACFALL: No, it does not, I am still of the opinion.

The two further witnesses as to medical matters were Dr Hugh Pierce and William Henry Roberts. Dr Pierce gave evidence which in essentials supported that of MacFall:

COUNSEL: About ten to twelve on the night of January 20th, you went to 29 Wolverton Street?

PIERCE: I did.

COUNSEL: And you saw the body of the deceased woman?

PIERCE: Yes.

COUNSEL: And you made a general examination?

PIERCE: Yes.

COUNSEL: What conclusion did you come to as to the time of death?

PIERCE: Well the fact that the hands and feet were cold proved to me that death had been some few hours previous to that.

COUNSEL: What do you mean by some few hours?

PIERCE: Taking all things into consideration, I thought death had taken place about six o'clock or maybe after.

COUNSEL: Did you examine the body subsequently?

PIERCE: Yes, periodically.

COUNSEL: How often?

PIERCE: Roughly every quarter of an hour or twenty minutes.

COUNSEL: Did you note the progress of rigor mortis?

PIERCE: Naturally, of course.

COUNSEL: You went in again at 12.25 I understand.

PIERCE: Yes.

COUNSEL: What did you see then?

PIERCE: Rigor mortis was very little different. The upper arm was getting slightly more rigid.

COUNSEL: A little later did you notice any difference?

PIERCE: The lower part of the right arm had become rigid.

COUNSEL: Were there any other facts which helped you to judge the time of death?

PIERCE: No. I simply went there to examine for rigor mortis because Professor MacFall asked me to.

COUNSEL: You simply took the rigor mortis?

PIERCE: Yes.

COUNSEL: As the rigor mortis progressed and you saw the body, did you come to any other conclusion than your previous one as to the time of death?

PIERCE: No.

MR JUSTICE WRIGHT: You mean you still thought it was about six o'clock or probably later?

PIERCE: Yes, my Lord.

COUNSEL: Can you say as to your limits? You say about six o'clock. What limits on either side of that would you give?

PIERCE: I would give two hours limit on either side.

MR JUSTICE WRIGHT: It might have been between four and eight?

PIERCE: Yes, my Lord.

COUNSEL: Would you say that death could not possibly have occurred after eight o'clock?

PIERCE: I would say definitely it could not have occurred after eight o'clock.

Dr Pierce agreed with Roland Oliver's cross-examination that taking the rectal temperature was a better test than rigor mortis. He also agreed that death could have taken place between four and eight pm.

William Henry Roberts, analyst for the city of Liverpool, gave evidence. Regarding the mackintosh he said that he would not expect an assailant who was naked while striking the blows to get a great deal of blood on his person. He did not think that there would be a lot of blood on his hands or his legs. There were no stains on the cash box or the dollar bill, neither were there blood stains on any other clothes in the house. This combined with the fact that there were no signs of blood on the towels in the bathroom or on the bedding in the front bedroom may well indicate that the attempt to create an impression of theft preceded the murder.

As is common in criminal trials the defence called their own medical witnesses to counter those of the prosecution. For the defence Professor James Edward Dible was called. Dible was a fellow of the Royal College of Surgeons and a Professor of Pathology at Liverpool University. He criticised MacFall for not having made any written notes of his examination and emphasised the likely inaccuracy of the rigor mortis test as compared with the rectal temperature method. Nevertheless, as to the precise hour of death he could only speak in general terms:

OLIVER: Your evidence comes to this, that judging as well as you can from the material before you, death might have occurred after seven o'clock?

DIBLE: Yes.

OLIVER: But you cannot say with any degree of certainty when it took place on these materials?

DIBLE: No.

Where does the medical evidence leave us? One suspects that it left the members of the jury completely mystified. Surely, it carried the case no further for Wallace or against him.

Now let us pause, before dealing with the police investigation which culminated with the arrest of Wallace, and consider the position of the jury. The absence of any blood on any of the clothes of Wallace created a difficulty for the Crown. But is the alternative scenario presented by the defence any more likely? The case for the defence is this:

A mystery figure, who is aware of Wallace's address and occupation, in fact who is entirely unknown to him and driven by a motive which has no rational explanation, forms a plan to induce Wallace to leave his house so that he, the unknown individual, can gain access and murder Julia Wallace for a reason which is completely obscure, and which no one, not least Wallace himself, can begin to explain. The evening before the murder this homicidal predator lurks somewhere outside the Wallace household keeping watch, yet, without any certainty whatever that Wallace will be leaving his house that night or at what time. He does not know whether Wallace will leave from the front or back entrance, but somehow manages to keep both under observation. When Wallace leaves he somehow manages to get to the telephone box at the junction of Breck Road and Rochester Road in time to see Wallace reach the corner of Richmond Park and Breck Road, and turn left at the corner. Then, without any certainty that Wallace is going to the central chess club he telephones the club and leaves a false message. He has to guarantee that Wallace will receive the message, and if received will act upon it.

The next night, again without any guarantee that Wallace will go looking for Menlove Gardens East, he again keeps watch at 29 Wolverton Street, armed with a heavy metal object and within a very short time of Wallace leaving the house, this person somehow talks Julia Wallace into admitting him into the premises. This, notwithstanding her husband's direction not to admit anyone into their home in his absence.

Having subjected the poor woman to a murderous and motiveless assault he attempts to create a disarray suggestive of a burglary – yet without leaving a trace of blood and with a total haul of £4. Finally having worn Wallace's mackintosh to commit the murder, he attempts to burn the mackintosh – which from his point of view would seem to be quite pointless. Finally with blood on his lower legs and shoes, and carrying the weapon, he leaves 29 Wolverton Street and makes his way to his own home.

CHAPTER SEVEN

INVESTIGATION AND ARREST

When Detective Superintendent Hubert Moore took charge of the investigation a little after 10pm on 20 January he displayed a vigorous approach to solving the case. Over the years many criticisms have been levelled both at Moore and the Liverpool City Police. It will be appropriate at this point to consider these disparaging allegations: how valid they are and the extent to which police inefficiency was the cause of the case never being solved.

First, let us look at Moore himself. Moore was, by any standards, a most experienced, able and energetic senior police officer. An Irishman by birth and a devout Roman Catholic, he had 30 years of experience in the police.

Initially, much of his work had involved countering Sein Fein activity in Liverpool, a city with a large catholic Irish population. Many of these people, while not approving of the violent tactics of the IRA nevertheless shared their hope for the ultimate independence of Ireland. A few, however, gave active assistance to extremists. Moore, while no doubt feeling some sympathy with the ideals of Irish nationalism, hated the men of violence for the criminal methods which they used to gain their ends, and thought that their tactics would have a reverse effect from what they intended and hoped for.

Moore won a lot of credit for his battle with the extremist element in Liverpool and at the end of 1930 he finally became head of the Liverpool CID. As such the Wallace case presented a serious challenge to his reputation, which he was anxious to preserve. However, hunting down terrorists was a very different test of his talents to solving a particularly problematic murder case, and to some extent, required different talents. A contemporary photograph of Moore shows a well dressed and well set up man complete with smart overcoat, wing collar and bowler hat. He is sporting an elegant moustache and his face bears all the marks of an intelligent, vigorous and, very much, no nonsense type of individual.

On his arrival at 29 Wolverton Street, Moore was spoken to by PC Williams who described his search of the house and the condition of the various rooms. Moore himself made a search of the house, which was no more successful than that made by Williams. However, there are two points of importance to make. First, Moore found that there were no signs of a forced entry. This was not challenged by the defence counsel and it was made clear that if Wallace was innocent then the murderer was admitted to the premises by Julia, and that person was someone who knew that Wallace was an agent of the Prudential. To that extent the field of suspects was starting to narrow.

The second important factor about the search of the house by Moore is that even in this early stage in his investigation Moore formed the view that the 'burglary' was not a genuine one. He was sure that the disorder in the front bedroom, the missing £4 from the cash box and the broken door, which had been wrenched off a cupboard, were attempts to give the impression that the murder had been committed in the course of a burglary. This was a conclusion to which Moore and his police colleagues came in due course and which led to suspicion culminating in the arrest of Wallace. Moore contacted other police stations and gave instructions that various clubs, railways stations, public houses and such-like should be searched, in the quest for a man with blood on his clothing. The result was negative.

Wallace himself supplied the police with names of people who Julia would have admitted to the house and taken into the front 'parlour'. These were relatives, their few friends or work colleagues of Wallace. He also stated unequivocally that he did not suspect any of these of murdering his wife. It was only after his final release that he claimed to know the identity of the killer, and well after his death that the name of Richard Gordon Parry came into the picture.

When a murder by means of a blunt instrument has taken place, one of the primary tasks for the police is to locate, if possible, the weapon used. If this is found it may yield useful clues. There may be fingerprints or traces of blood, it could be possible to trace its origin and locate the supplier or previous owner. In the Wallace mystery the terrible injuries to the head suffered by Julia make it clear that some such weapon was used. Nevertheless, the instrument of death was never found. However, some light was shed upon the matter by Mrs Jane Sarah Draper. For some nine months she had been working as a cleaner for the Wallace's, visiting their house once a week. Her last visit had been on January 7, a short while before the date of the murder.

Detective Inspector Gold who, with detective Sergeant Harry Bailey, was assisting in the enquiry, asked Mrs Draper to look round the kitchen and also the rest of the house to see if there was anything with which she was familiar which was missing. Mrs Draper found that two items were missing. One was a small poker. This was a light object and had been kept in the kitchen, The other, of greater interest, was an iron bar. This, Mrs Draper said, had been kept in the parlour during the whole time in which she had been visiting number 29. It had either been kept standing by the fireplace or laid underneath the kerb. It was used to clean underneath the gas fire. She said she had seen it on the 7 January. She had used it to retrieve a screw which had fallen and rolled underneath the fire.

The police made an exhaustive search for the suspect weapon but without result. When the matter was put to Wallace he replied 'she must have thrown the poker away with the ashes. I don't know anything about the piece of iron in the parlour'. Shown a replica at the trial, Professor MacFall said that just such a weapon would produce the injuries suffered by Julia Wallace. One thing is certain. The iron bar could have been the instrument of murder, and it was removed from the house after the death of Julia Wallace. Apart from that, the rest – who used it and how it was disposed of – is supposition. Two incidents deserve special attention. These are the evidence of Lily Hall which has been touched upon, and the conversation Wallace had with Beattie and another during the period of the police enquiry. Lily was a young typist who claimed to have known Wallace by sight for three or four years, Julia Wallace had been a member of the congregation at Holy Trinity Church. Lily and her mother were also regular worshipers and sometimes spoke with Mrs Wallace after the service. Lily gave her evidence in the trial:

HALL: I have known the accused by sight for three or four years. I last saw him on January 20th at the bottom of the entry to Richmond Park.

What time was that?

HALL: About twenty to nine at night.

Was Mr Wallace alone there?

HALL: No.

Who was he with?

HALL: Talking to a man.

Could you see them quite clearly?

HALL: Yes.

Was it light there?

HALL: There was a lamp further along.

As you crossed over to Letchworth street, what was the last thing you saw?

HALL: They parted.

And where had they gone?

HALL: One went straight along and one down the entry.

Could you see which one went down the entry and which one went along Breck Road?

HALL: No.

Have you any doubt about it being the accused?

HALL: No.

Cross-examination by Roland Oliver KC:

OLIVER: How often did you seen him?

HALL: Not very often.

OLIVER: I suppose you saw a good many other people about the streets?

HALL: Yes.

OLIVER: You never gave those a thought at the time did you?

HALL: No.

OLIVER: No, why should you? Then there was a murder. How long after the murder did you give your statement to the police?

HALL: I think it was about a week, but I am not quite sure.

Goodman (in *The Killing of Julia Wallace*) raises four points which should prove Lily Hall was mistaken:

First, in spite of police appeals the other man to whom Wallace was said to be speaking failed to respond. This, however is hardly surprising, Even though there may have been nothing suspicious in the meeting the missing potential witness would have known that Wallace was the subject of a murder enquiry and not have wished to get involved.

Secondly, why should Wallace have told a deliberate lie when it was obvious that he must have seen her? This was a dark January evening, he may not have seen her if he was engrossed in his conversation.

Thirdly, Lily was confused over the direction in which she was walking to go to the cinema. Lily was giving evidence concerning events three months previously.

Fourthly, although she could not have been more than 10 yards away from the two men when they parted she was, at that time, unable to identify one man from the other. Police arranged an identification parade nearer the time at which Lily immediately picked out Wallace as the man she saw that night.

Roland Oliver, as was his proper duty, challenged Miss Hall's identification. He did so by employing a familiar advocate's tactic of attacking flaws in evidence as a basis for claiming that the whole of it was worthless. What the jury thought we do not know, but sometimes an honest but confused witness can make a better impression than a smooth and skilful liar.

In his statement to the police of 29 January Wallace said of this episode:

As far as I can recollect I do not know anyone named Hall living in the neighbourhood of Wolverton Street, or Richmond Park, or any of the streets adjacent, but I have an idea that I have heard my late wife mention someone of that name in connection with Holy Trinity Church, but my recollection of that is very hazy.

It has never been suggested that Wallace acted with an accomplice in a plan to murder his wife, but if Lily was telling the truth then Wallace was lying. He may have done so because what she had seen was inconsistent with his account that he hurried home that night.

The second matter of interest took place on 22 January at about 10.20pm. Samuel Beattie and James Caird were leaving the chess club when they encountered Wallace, who was looking pale and drawn. Wallace said to Beattie: 'Oh, that telephone message, can you remember definitely what time you actually received the message?' Beattie replied: 'Well, seven or shortly after'. Wallace replied: 'Cannot you get a bit nearer than that?' Beattie said:'I am sorry but I cannot'. Wallace replied: 'Well, it is important to me, and I should like to know if you can get nearer to it than that'. Beattie said: 'Well, I am sorry but I cannot'. Wallace then said: 'I have just left the police, they have cleared me'. Beattie expressed satisfaction at the news.

The immediate question has to be – if Wallace had been cleared why was he still so concerned about the telephone call? Clearance would mean that the police had made a definite decision that Wallace was no longer a suspect and had informed him of this. No such thing had happened.

On 20 January Wallace made his full statement of defence. It was the story he adhered to for the rest of his life:

I am 52 years and by occupation an insurance agent for the Prudential Insurance Company, Dale Street. I have resided at 29 Wolverton Street with my wife Julia (deceased) age believed 52 years, for the past 16 years. There are no children of the marriage. My wife and I have been on the best of terms all our married life. At 10.30am today I left the house, leaving my wife indoors doing her household duties. I went on my insurance round in Clubmoor district, my last call being 177 Lisburne Lane shortly before 2pm. I then took a tram car to Trinity Church, Breck Road arriving at my house at 2.10pm. My wife was then well and I had dinner and left the house at about 3.15pm. I then returned to Clubmoor and continued my collections and finished about 5.55pm. My last call being either 19 or 21 Eastman Road. I boarded a bus at Queens Drive and Townsend Avenue, alighted at College Hall, and walked up to my house at about 6.05pm. I entered my house by the back door which is my usual practice, and then had tea with my wife, who was quite well and then I left the house at 6.45pm leaving by the back door. I caught a car from Belmont Road and West Derby Road and got off at Lodge Lane and Smithdown Road and boarded a Smithdown Road car to Penny Lane. I then boarded another car up Menlove Avenue West, looking for Menlove Gardens East where I had an appointment with Mr R M Qualtrough for 7.30 in connection with my insurance business. I was unable to find the address and I enquired at Menlove Avenue West and I also asked at the bottom of Green Lane, Allerton, a constable about the address, he told me there was no such address. I then called at a post office near the Plaza Cinema to look at the directory, but there was none there, and I was unable to find the address. I also visited a newsagent where there was a directory but I was unable to find the address. It was then 8pm and I caught a tram car to Lodge Lane and then a car to West Derby Road and Belmont Road and walked home from there.

I arrived at Wolverton Street about 8.45pm and I pulled out my key, and went to open the front door and found it secure and could not open it with my key. I knocked gently but got no answer. I could not see any light in the house. I then went around to the back, the door leading from the entry to the back yard was closed, but not bolted. I went to the back door of the house and was unable to get in. I do not know if the door was bolted or not, it sticks sometimes, but I think the door was bolted but I am not sure. There was a small light on in the back kitchen, but no light in the kitchen. I then went back to the front. I was suspicious because I expected my wife to be in, and the light in the kitchen. I tried my key in the front door again, and found the lock did not work properly. The key would turn in it, but seemed to unturn without unlocking the door. I rushed around to the back and saw my neighbours Mr and Mrs Johnston, coming out of 31 Wolverton Street. I said to them have you heard any suspicious noise in my house in the past hours or so? Mrs Johnston said they hadn't. I said then I couldn't get in and asked them if they would wait a while, while I tried again. I then found the back door opened quite easily. I walked in by the back kitchen door. I found the kitchen light, I lit it and found signs of disturbance in the kitchen, A wooden case in which I keep photographic stuff had been broken open and the lid was on the floor. I then went upstairs and entered the middle bedroom, but saw nothing unusual. I then entered the bathroom, but it was correct. I then entered the back room and found no disturbance there. I then entered the front room, struck a match, and found the bed upset, the clothes being off. I don't think my wife left it like that. I then came down and looked into the front room, after striking a match, and saw my wife lying on the floor. I felt her hand and confirmed that she was dead. I then rushed out and told Mr and Mrs Johnston what had happened, saying something but I cannot remember what I did say. After my neighbours had been in Mr Johnston went for the police and a doctor. I asked him to go. I afterwards found that £4 had been taken from a cashbox in the kitchen, but I am not sure of the amount. When I discovered my wife lying on the floor I noticed my mackintosh lying on the floor at the back of her. I wore the mackintosh up to today but left it off owing to the fine weather. My wife has never worn a mackintosh to my knowledge. You drew my attention to it being burnt, but it was not like that when I last saw it and I can't explain it. I have no suspicion of anyone.

William Herbert Wallace

The body of Julia Wallace, having been officially identified by her sister-in-law, Amy, was taken to the Princes Mortuary, but the police, notwithstanding all their efforts, had drawn a blank. They have been criticised by writers on the case, and at the time the public, who were becoming increasingly aware of the drama, were eager for an arrest. They remained frustrated and puzzled. The house at 29 Wolverton Street had been thoroughly searched, without any real clues having been obtained; scores of potential suspects who would or could have been admitted to the house were questioned and their alibis checked; numerous items such as clothes and various utensils sent for examination at the forensic laboratory; the area combed for the murder weapon, but all to no effect. Moore and his colleagues Bailey and Gold held a number of conferences and Wallace himself was interviewed several times without progress. Confronted with such a conundrum Moore felt that the reputation of himself and his officers was at stake. Some of the disparagement however was not entirely unjustified. Superintendent Moore and his team overlooked several basic matters which could have made the case against Wallace stronger, or helped to establish his innocence. Too little attention was paid to the usual route Wallace took when he visited the chess club. No attempt was made to contact the conductor of the tram which took Wallace to the club on the Monday night. The times were vital in the question of whether or not he could have made the telephone call.

Worse still, officers were allowed to wander round the house interfering with items which might have contained vital fingerprints, such as the cash box from which the £4 was missing and the notes found in the ornament in the middle bedroom. Professor MacFall, the main medical witness for the police failed to apply the correct test to determine the time of death. In addition there was no proper examination made of Julia Wallace's Medical history. A much more thorough check should have been made of the buses and trams on the 19th and 20th on the routes used by Wallace including when they stopped and left their various stages.

Some of the complaints seem groundless. Robert F Hussey in his work *Murderer Scot-Free* (David & Charles, 1972) states:

A fixed idea mentality overshadowed all police work, from Superintendent Moore down to the greenest constable, the police were determined to convict Wallace, even if it meant closing their eyes and minds to every other possibility.

The fact is that the police only decided to charge Wallace after they were satisfied that they had eliminated every other possible suspect.

It was only long after the dismissal of the case against him, that Wallace claimed to know the identity of the murderer. At the time of Moore's investigation Wallace confirmed that there was no one whom he suspected of having committed the crime. On Monday 2 February, the Director of Police Prosecutions, after some initial hesitation, agreed that there was a case for Wallace to answer. At 7.00pm Superintendents Moore and Thomas accompanied by Inspector Gold visited Wallace at 83 Ullet Road. 'You know who I am' said Gold to Wallace. Wallace replied 'Yes'. 'William Herbert Wallace' said Gold 'it is my duty to arrest you on the charge of the wilful murder of your wife, Julia Wallace on the night of the 20th January 1931 at 29 Wolverton Street'. A shaken Wallace having been cautioned, replied 'What can I say to this charge of which I am entirely innocent'.

CHAPTER 8

WILLIAM HERBERT WALLACE ON TRIAL

In the earlier part of this work I have thought it proper to quote extensively from the transcript of the trial as recorded by W F Wyndham-Brown in his book *The Trial of William Herbert Wallace* (Gollancz, 1933). This is because I have felt it better that the reader should be able to form his or her views on the basis of the evidence on which the court reached its decision rather than on the various opinions of previous writers. In this chapter I shall avoid repetition of ground already covered, by confining my scope to a precis of much of the testimony already referred to. We shall look in more detail, however, at the strategy of the prosecution and the defence and in particular the evidence-in-chief and the cross examination of Wallace himself.

The personalities of counsel, the speeches to the jury and the interventions and the summing up by the judge will also be the subject of study.

The tribunal before which the life of William Wallace hung in the balance was the Liverpool Spring Assizes of 1931 held at St George's Hall, Liverpool on Wednesday 22 April 1931. A jury of 12 people were sworn in to decide the guilt or innocence of the defendant, in those days commonly referred to as 'the accused' or 'the prisoner', but now named 'the defendant'. The judge was Mr Justice Wright and the counsel were the Recorder of Liverpool for the crown, Mr Edward George Hemmerde KC together with Mr Leslie Walsh and Mr Roland Oliver KC and Mr S Scholefield Allen on behalf of the defendant. Let us, before we take a closer look at the leading personalities in this now famous legal drama, reflect on the nature of the judicial body which held the future of Wallace in its hands, and see how it compares with the court of today.

The courts of Assizes were periodic criminal courts held around England and Wales until 1972, when, together with the quarter sessions, they were abolished by the Courts Act 1971 and replaced by a simple, permanent Crown Court. The Assizes heard the most serious cases which were committed to it by the Quarter Sessions (local county courts held four times a year), while more minor offences were dealt with summarily by Justices of the Peace in petty sessions (also known as magistrates' courts).

The word 'assizes' refers to the sittings or sessions (old French: assesses) of the judges known as 'Justices of Assize', who were judges of the Kings Bench Division of the High Courts of Justice who travelled across the seven circuits of England on Commissions of Oyer and the Terminer (to hear and determine) setting up court and summoning juries at the various assize towns.

An Act passed in the reign of King Edward I provided that writs summoning juries to Westminster were to appoint a time and place for hearing the causes of the county of origin. Thus they were known as writs of *Nisi Prius* (Latin: unless before). The jury would hear the case at Westminster unless the King's Justices had assembled a court in the county to deal with the case beforehand. The commission of Oyer and Terminer was a general commission to hear and determine cases, while the commission of gaol delivery required the justices to try all persons held in the jail.

Few substantial changes occurred until the nineteenth century. From the 1830s onwards Wales and the Palatine county of Chester, previously served by the court of Grand Session, were merged into the circuit system. The commission for London and Middlesex were replaced with a Central Criminal Court, serving the whole metropolis and county courts were established around the country to hear many civil cases previously covered by *Nisi Prius*.

The Supreme Court of Judicature Act 1873, which created the Supreme Court of Judicature, transferred the jurisdiction of the Commissions of Assize to the High Court of Justice and established district registers of the High Court across the country, further diminishing the civil jurisdiction of the Assizes. In 1956 Crown Courts were set up in Liverpool and Manchester, replacing the Assizes and Quarter Sessions. This was extended nationwide in 1972, following the recommendation of a Royal Commission.

The central feature of English criminal trials, above the level of the magistrates' courts is the jury. The jury system, which is almost unknown in continental countries, is rooted in the English trust in the common sense of the common citizen. Rather than rely upon the expertise of a panel of experts, or a bench of judges or a single judge, questions of fact are felt to be safer in the hands of a group of ordinary people, for them to apply their good sense and experience of life. The Mountbatten Committee recommended specially qualified jurors to hear cases of great complexity such as complicated fraud matters, but the idea has never met with general acceptance.

The English jury has its roots in two institutions that date from before the Norman Conquest in 1066. The inquest, as a means of settling a fact, had developed in Scandinavia and the Carolingian Empire, while Anglo-Saxon law had used a 'jury of accusation' to establish the strength of an allegation against a criminal suspect. In the latter case the jury were not tryers of fact, and if the accusation was such as posing a case to answer, guilt or innocence was established by oath, often in the form of compurgation or trial by ordeal. During the 11th and 12th centuries juries were sworn to decide property disputes but it was the Roman Catholic Church's withdrawal of support for trial by ordeal that necessitated the development of the jury in it's modern form.

Juries are summoned for criminal trials in the Crown Court where the offence is an indictable offence or an offence triable either way that has been sent to the Crown Court after an examination by magistrates. Magistrates have the power to send an indictable offence triable either way to the Crown Court, but even if they elect to try it themselves, the accused retains the right to elect for a Crown Court with a jury. Summary offences are tried by magistrates and there is no right of Crown Court trial by jury. Only recently, during this century, has the principle been constituted in law that juries may be dispensed with where there has been tampering or there is a danger of tampering with a jury, and it would be in the interests of justice that a single judge sitting alone should try the case. Another development in recent times has been the introduction of majority verdicts. If a jury returns and informs the judge that it cannot reach a unanimous verdict, the judge may send them out to try again. However if they are still unable to reach agreement then he may accept a decision by a majority of the jury. This must be on the basis of eleven to one, ten to two, and ten to one or nine to one if, for any reason the number of jury men and women has been reduced below twelve (Juries Act 1974).

In criminal trials every effort is made to ensure that the members of the jury are not prejudiced either for or against the defendant at the start of the trial. They must set aside all preconceived views and ideas and decide solely on the evidence which they have heard in court. In his summing up the judge will remind them forcibly of this. Normally counsel will do the same. This can be an optimistic exercise. Where the case has gained wide spread publicity it becomes common knowledge, and therefore the subject of much discussion in the area of the crime, if not considerably beyond it. Not every juror, when sworn in, will see fit to disclose what he or she may well regard as a harmless chat with a friend or neighbour on the subject. There are reasons to believe that this was so in the Wallace case.

Other changes have taken place in criminal trials since 1931. For example, it is now mandatory for the prosecution to supply the defence with the statements of those witnesses which the prosecution do not intend to call. Equally, there is an obligation upon the defence to supply the crown with advance notice of an alibi which the defendant is planning to put forward. The greatest change which alters the very heavy sense of terrible responsibility the jury must have felt has been the abolition of capital punishment. It is incredible to recall that as late as 1832 one could be hanged for shoplifting goods worth five shillings or less and that public executions only ended in 1868.

After the Second World War ended, several executions took place which caused great public concern. These, such as the hanging of Timothy Evans in 1966 and Derek Bentley in 1968 resulted in posthumous pardons. There were many who doubted that the convictions were justified. In 1861 the number of capital crimes was reduced to four: murder, treason, arson in the Royal Dock Yards and piracy with violence.

Following a Private Members Bill in 1965, Parliament voted to suspend the death penalty for five years. Since the beginning of the century capital punishment had been the only sentence a judge could pass for the crime of murder. A jury could add to its verdict a 'recommendation to mercy', but the Home Secretary could accept or reject this. There lay an appeal to the Court of Criminal Appeal but this was limited to a few categories such as the judge misdirecting the jury on matters of fact or law. The Attorney General could refer the case to the House of Lords (judicial body), but only if the appeal contained important points of law. It will be seen that the verdict of the appeal court in the Wallace case broke new ground in this respect.

If the Home Secretary accepted the recommendation to mercy the sentence of death would be commuted to life imprisonment; this would hardly be available to Wallace after such a brutal homicide.

On the 20 May 1998, during a debate on the Human Rights Bill, members of Parliament decided by 294 to 136 to adopt the provisions of the European Convention on Human Rights outlawing capital punishment for murder 'except in times of war or imminent threat of war'. The Bill incorporates the European Convention on Human Rights into British law. On the 31 July 1998, the Criminal Justice Bill removed high treason and piracy with violence as capital crimes, thus effectively ending capital punishment. On 27 January 1999 the Home Secretary formally signed the Sixth Protocol of the European Convention of Human Rights in Strasbourg, on behalf of the British Government, formally abolishing the death penalty in the United Kingdom. In years past, a defendant could only succeed with a plea of insanity when his or her mental condition fell within the MacNaughton rules. Today the defence of diminished responsibility has a wider application.

When Wallace entered the dock on the 22 April 1931 the death penalty, if one may mix ones metaphors, was very much alive.

Now let us take a look at the very distinguished lawyers who played their part in a unique legal drama.

Mr Justice Wright, the judge in the case, was a man of extraordinary brilliance. Robert Anderson Wright was one of the very greatest lawyers and jurists in Britain. He was born in 1869, was called to the Bar in 1900 and became Kings Counsel in 1917. He became a bencher of the Inner Temple in 1923 and a judge of the Kings Bench division of the High Court of Justice in 1925 at the early age of 56. He had tried a number of criminal cases, but he was particularly expert in the field of commercial law. In 1932, he was promoted directly to the House of Lords as a Lord of Appeal in Ordinary taking the title of Lord Wright of Durley. He later became Master of the Rolls from 1935 to 1937 and in due course Chairman of the United Nations War Crimes Commission in 1945. He continued to serve in the House of Lords until his retirement at the age of 78. He died in 1964.

It is perhaps unfortunate that Mr Justice Wright wanted the case to be over in four days so that he could complete his schedule of sitting in other courts. Whether this gave an unfair advantage to the prosecution is debatable. One thing is certain, his conduct of the case was impeccable, accurate, precise and courteous. He never evinced any sign that he was leaning towards one side or the other, and his summing up was, without question, in Wallace's favour.

Edward George Hemmerde KC, the recorder of Liverpool, was briefed to lead for the Crown. Hemmerde had for many years been a controversial and colourful character in Liverpool. That he was also a man of brilliance and enormous energy cannot be disputed. As a young man at Oxford he had excelled at sport, winning the Henley Diamond Sculls in 1900. He was handsome and of first class physique, qualities he retained well into middle age, but he had a high pitched voice which became shrill when he was excited. He was called to the Bar and subsequently 'took silk' at the same time as two other men, also of exceptional ability, F E Smith and John Simon. His early years at the Bar were ones of unbroken success, but there was an element of unpleasant egotism, even exhibitionism, about him which was already attracting criticism at the time of the Wallace case.

Not content with a very busy practice at the Bar he decided to enter politics and was elected Liberal Member of Parliament for East Denbigh in 1906, at the early age of 35. In 1909, the Liberal government nominated him

Recorder of Liverpool. This, although a judicial office, did not necessitate him abandoning his practice as a barrister. On top of all this, Hemmerde co-operated in the writing of several plays one of which *A Butterfly on the Wheel* ran for 119 performances.

Then things began to go wrong. Like some other men of outstanding gifts, Hemmerde suffered a lack of stability in his own affairs. Notwithstanding his substantial earnings as a successful barrister, a Recorder, Member of Parliament and playwright, Hemmerde had interests which landed him in financial difficulties. He was a gambler who, having lost at the roulette wheel, and worse still the Stock Exchange, began the fatal course of borrowing money. In 1921 he was sued over a debt of £1,000 (more like £20,000 in today's money) and foolishly, instead of settling the matter out of court, decided to make a legal battle of it. Having lost in the initial court hearing he won on appeal but lost again in the House of Lords. He suffered severely, not merely financially but in the damage done to his reputation. This was only the start of his misfortunes. In the midst of his struggles with debt his wife divorced him, and in spite of changing his allegiance to Labour and winning a seat for his new party he was passed over for a Law Officership. Then followed the terrible news that his only son had been killed in an accident while in East Africa. In addition to all of this, he quarrelled with the Liverpool City Council and with its leader Sir Thomas White, with the result that for years he never received an important brief from the Liverpool Corporation.

At the time of the Wallace case Hemmerde's career was badly in need of resuscitation. When he received the brief for the Crown in the Wallace case he was delighted – just as some others were surprised. It was his chance to re-establish his professional reputation.

Roland Gifford Oliver KC, counsel for Wallace, could not have been a more different type of man from Hemmerde, both in his personality and his style of advocacy. Roland Gifford Oliver was born in 1882. He took silk in 1925. Seven years after the Wallace trial he was appointed a Knight and elevated as a judge of the High Court. He retired in 1957 and died a year later at the age of 76.

In the year of Wallace's trial, 1931, Oliver was one of the best known and most highly respected barristers in the country. He was also one of the most experienced. He had appeared in a number of famous cases. It should be remembered that in those days, before television, leading barristers received almost as much public attention as prominent footballers and media celebrities do today. It is also true to say that the same could be said of colourful murder trials. In the present time the newspapers are so full of murders and various forms of violence that the details are read and forgotten before the following day's edition. In the 1920s and 1930s one single case could dominate the news for weeks, if not months. Great advocates such as Marshall Hall, Sir Patrick Hastings and Norman Birkett were national figures to an extent far beyond any Queen's Counsel today.

Oliver had a wide-ranging practice which included civil and divorce cases in addition to murder cases, and he frequently prosecuted as well as defended the occupants of the dock. He had been junior counsel to famous prosecutor Richard Muir, in the Steinie Morrison murder case in 1911, and in 1921 he was led by the Solicitor General, Sir Thomas Inskip, in the historic Thompson-Bywaters trial, which resulted in the highly controversial execution of Edith Thompson, one of the last women to be hanged in England. (The horror of her fate did much to undermine the belief of Parliament in the death penalty.) For the defence, Oliver had been junior to a giant-like Marshall Hall whose string of successes in defending celebrated cases of murder were achieved by an emotional and electrifying style of addressing juries which has never been equalled since. Yet Oliver's style was anything but florid. A contemporary photograph discloses a face both intense and calm. There was something precise and calculating about him. Not for him the ultra aggressive cross-examinations or the passionate speech. A rational appeal and well reasoned argument were his weapons, and they could be very effective. Nevertheless, his defence of Wallace received a great deal of criticism, and there is no doubt he made a few avoidable mistakes in his conduct of the trial as counsel for the defence. These we shall note in the rest of this chapter.

Hector Munro, Wallace's solicitor, seems to have thought that Oliver's quiet approach and rational appeal would "cut down to size" the prosecution assault. Was this a mistake? Many thought that it was. Jonathan Goodman in *The Killing of Julia Wallace* says this of him:

> Although among fellow members of the Bar, Oliver was generally respected and admired for the sharpness and clarity of his legal mind, and for his ability to grasp complicated facts and communicate them, simplified but undistorted, to judges and juries, there were few people who found him likable as a person. He was a cold, austere apparently unemotional man who carried the atmosphere of the courtroom around with him as a snail carries its shell, no matter whether he was questioning a witness in court or conversing with a companion at the dinner table, his speech was almost entirely free of contradictions – he would invariably say "Is it not?" "Never I don't." His faced was lined, but not as a result of laughter, for there were not many things that amused him – least of all jokes concerning the law. The law was his religion;

the statute book his bible; the law was majestic, well-nigh perfect, almost almighty – or so he believed.

Paradoxically, if he had slightly less respect for the law, he would have achieved far greater success as a jury advocate. Whereas the great defenders – men like Marshall Hall, Curtis Bennett and Hastings – used the law as a guide line, letting go of it if they saw a chance of taking a legitimate short cut to a winning verdict, Oliver used the law as if it were a tight rope stretched from the beginning of a case to the end; at times was he so intent upon keeping his balance that he failed to notice what his opponents were up to.

Oliver and Hemmerde were both the subject of complaint about the way they conducted themselves in the Wallace trial – but for very different reasons. Hemmerde was criticised for being too enthusiastic in presenting the case for the Crown. In his speeches, it was said, he spoke to the jury as though the case against Wallace had been proved; as though it was 'watertight' whereas in fact it contained many weak points. He was condemned in the minds of some for his alleged 'bulldozing' style, and the fact that he failed to follow the English tradition that the prosecutor, unlike the defender, does not indulge in histrionics or dramatic gestures, but lays out his case in a calm and dispassionate manner. It is an unwritten rule of advocacy, peculiarly English, that prosecuting counsel does not strive to obtain a conviction, still less to suggest to the court what the appropriate penalty should be.

There is another firm forensic principle; namely that a barrister must never, either expressly or by implication, betray his or her personal belief or disbelief in the case that they are obliged to advance. To the old question: 'How can you defend someone who you know to be guilty' the answer must be, 'I don't know them to be guilty or innocent, that is for the court to decide'. This is not a matter of shifting responsibility for the decision and its consequences, which in the days of capital punishment and the absence of the verdict of diminished responsibility could be a very heavy burden for the jury. It is simply the nature of the barrister's profession, though this may not be easy for a layperson to appreciate.

Robert F Hussey in his book *Murderer Scott-Free* censures Hemmerde for the conduct of his case:

> In self justification, therefore, if not desperation for reinstatement of former status, Hemmerde clearly went all out for a conviction with an extreme vehemence, almost vindictiveness that Britons deplore, that American's increasingly frown upon.

> It is quite probable that having seen at the outset the weakness of his proofs as supplied by the Liverpool Solicitor and having realised that nothing really conclusive existed beyond the habitual suspicion against any husband in a wife murder case, the wily Hemmerde decided to adopt a policy of piling

suspicion upon suspicion in the hope that sheer quantity of allegation and a biblical cloud of witnesses, would successfully cancel the absence of probative facts.

From the very outset we have seen in his opening speech how he overstated the evidence he promised to call. On point after point his manner from the beginning had been far from dispassionate in the approved style. He had sarcastically suggested: you may find it curious that ... or supposing you come to the conclusion that? or you can find a man pretending or why on earth should he? etc, etc; a long line of insinuations and adumbrations which he had promised the jury would carry them almost irresistibly to a conclusion of Wallace's guilt – guilt so much beyond any reasonable doubt that they would call him to account.

All through the development of the case Hemmerde's tactics continued to obscure the basic issues with expressed or implied disbelief of even the simplest act or word of the accused. He called thirty seven witnesses to dozens of 'facts' – many of them quite inconsequential facts, mere quantity was his goal. Aptly one barrister has written: if a display is elaborate enough, only the very strong minded are able to see that suspicion has not, by elaboration, become evidence.

Here again, there appears to be a degree of misunderstanding of the advocate's profession, in which is necessary to emphasise the strong points in his case and minimise, the weaker ones. This is not dishonesty; it is a strategy well within the ethics of the barristers work. It must be borne in mind that counsel on the other side will be doing the same thing. An intelligent jury should be able to distinguish a strong point from a weak one. Moreover, the summing up by the judge, while giving a firm direction to the jury that they are the judges of fact, can also properly assist them on this issue.

With regard to Oliver, the objection that he lacked conviction, to the extent of almost giving the impression that he disbelieved his client, is not well-founded either. As with other professions, a member of the Bar brings to his work the method and style which his or her personality can best express. This author can confirm from his own experience, that advocates, particularly at the Criminal Bar, vary greatly in this respect. One may address a jury in a volatile and mercurial manner; another more quietly and relying upon logical argument rather than a show of emotion. Sir Edward Marshall Hall is an example of the first, Sir Norman Birkett of the second. Which of the two is more effective will depend upon the skill of the advocate, the nature of the case and the reaction of the jury.

The feature of the Wallace case which makes it so unique is that so few of the facts are in dispute. The contest depends upon the interpretation of those facts and therein lay the difficulty. So much was left to supposition. There was so little of the prosecution evidence that Wallace denied, what he challenged was on matters where he could not easily be contradicted. He insisted that he did not know, and had never seen Lily Hall on the night of 20 January. It was a dark night and this was possible. He repudiated her evidence that he was speaking with someone. She was a very poor witness in court which made her account less likely. He claimed that he did not say to PC Williams that the back door was bolted, or that he had told Superintendent Moore that the front door was. Neither remark was noted down at the time they were spoken, and it is common knowledge that police officers, like others, can err over details of a conversation. Wallace maintained that he had never seen the suspect iron bar in the parlour nor had he a familiar knowledge of the Menlove Gardens district. He had visited his superior Crewe there and had passed through it with his wife, but this was some years before, when it was dark at the winter period.

The whole prosecution was based on a theory. Put simply the jury was presented with two accounts to choose from, the Crown and the Defence, and each one was as unlikely as the other.

And so the trial began, the Clerk of the Assize spoke the solemn words to a pale but controlled Wallace:

> Herbert William Wallace, you are indicted and the charge against you is murder, in that on the 20th January, 1931, at Liverpool, you murdered Julia Wallace. How say you William Herbert Wallace, are you guilty or not guilty?

The reply of the defendant was 'Not guilty'.

The Clerk of the Assize then made out the charge to the jury:

> Members of the jury, the prisoner at the Bar, William Herbert Wallace, is indicted and the charge against him is murder, in that on 20th January 1931, at Liverpool, he murdered Julia Wallace. Upon this indictment he has been arraigned, upon his arraignment he has pleaded that he is not guilty, and he has put himself upon his country, which country you are and it is for you to enquire whether he be guilty or not and to hearken to the evidence

A hush fell upon the court as Hemmerde rose to open the case for the crown. Hemmerde opened his case 'high' in fact very 'high'. This is a well-known expression in legal circles. In layperson's language the term might be translated as dogmatically, even optimistically. A critic would call it opening the case as though it had already been proved and that all that remained was to make this fact clear to the jury. Crown counsel are, however, obliged to explain why what they are suggesting to the jury would justify their convicting the defendant, and this involves making reference to the evidence which they expect their witnesses to give. This may be done in a more or less forceful manner, but counsel who made his statement in a half hearted way may give the impression that there is little strength in the prosecution. On the other hand a 'high' opening is not without its dangers. If a witness for the Crown fails to give the anticipated testimony or proves weak and unreliable under cross-examination then the prosecution arguments may suffer a degree of deflation which will not go unnoticed in the jury box.

As has been discussed, Hemmerde's career and reputation were in need of a boost, and a victory in a now famous murder trial would provide just that. Nevertheless, able and experienced barrister that he was, Hemmerde must have spotted the weak points in his case from the documents supplied to him and the information and instructions he received from the police and from his solicitor. It is clear from his opening speech that he had decided that his best strategy was to go onto the offensive from the start. He was, however, shrewd enough to make some concessions which should remove any impression of unfair bias. He began with a brief summary:

May it please your Lordship, members of the jury; the charge against the prisoner, as you have heard is murder. I shall have to open to you in some detail a story not without its difficulties [concession] but which I think [proper expression submit] must show a very serious case against the prisoner. He has been for some years an agent of the Prudential, and he was living at a house in Wolverton Street in Anfield in this city, and had been living there for some years with his wife, apparently on terms of happiness and comradeship. In fact, so far as the happiness of this household is concerned, the Crown knows nothing to the contrary of the view that these two people were very happy together. In spite of that, the Crown now lay before you evidence, which, though it will not show you any motive, nevertheless, I shall suggest to you [perfectly proper mode of address] will carry you almost to the irresistible conclusion that in spite of all the happiness of that little household, in spite of everything that one knows about the relations of these people, on the night of January 20th of this year this woman was murdered by her husband .

There were two things which had to be proved in order to convict Wallace. The first was that the telephone call to the chess club was made by Wallace himself. The second was that between the hours of 6.00pm and 6.45pm, the following day, Wallace murdered his wife.

Hemmerde went on to describe the message which 'Qualtrough' left for Wallace, the defendant's reaction when told and his decision to respond to the request next day. Hemmerde pointedly called attention to the fact that the telephone kiosk from which the call was made was only 400 yards from Wallace's house and that, but for a hiatus on the line, the police would never have found this out. He said that only members of the club would have known about the meetings for play, but failed to mention that there was a board, displaying the dates of matches and the persons involved.

Hemmerde then went on to pour scorn on what he assumed was the only alternative theory to Wallace himself being the murderer:

You may think it strange that a total stranger to the prisoner, speaking from a place four hundred yards from his house, where according to him, he actually was at the time, should have rung up the City Café; you would have thought he might have called at the house (to deliver false information! Hardly likely); you might think he would have written to the house, he might have left a note at the house. None of these things happened, but a person, unknown to the prisoner with the name Qualtrough rings up the City Café, where that chess club plays, and there leaves a message that he is expected the next night to call on someone he does not know, at an address which you will find does not exist. There is no Menlove Gardens East, and you will have to consider whether this giving of his name and address was part of a cunningly laid scheme to create an alibi for the next night, or whether it was really a genuine message.

Hemmerde spoke very briefly about the evidence of PC Rothwell and then came to the statement of Close (the Milkboy). Hemmerde knew only too well that he was on very dangerous ground for the prosecution here, He tried to skirt over this by an over-confident statement as to what Close would say, the manner in which he would say it and the accounts which other witnesses would give of the same episode:

At 6.30pm a boy called Close delivers milk at 29 Wolverton Street. He knows the time very accurately, because he had to go on foot that day; I think his bicycle was out of order, and he had to complete his round by a certain time, and he will tell you that he noticed the clock; according to him [not yet given in evidence!] it must have been within a minute or two one way or the other of half past six when he delivered the milk to 29 Wolverton Street and saw Mrs Wallace, the deceased woman and spoke to her. That was the last time that she was seen alive. We know that at that time, from Wallace's own statement he was there and apparently left the house somewhere about 6.45. You may take it that if in fact he is guilty of this atrocious crime – because whoever did it was guilty of a most atrocious crime – it must have been committed within the time from 6.30 to about 6.50 because at a time between 7.06 and 7.10 he boarded a car at the junction of Smithdown Lane and Lodge Lane – I say between 7.06 and 7.10 because sometimes the cars are running at that time about two minutes late and I give just the margin.

When Allan Close gave evidence at the trial he stated, very shortly, that on the night of the murder he delivered milk at the Wallace's home. It was taken in by Mrs Wallace and the time was 6.30pm. He stated that he knew the time because when he passed Holy Trinity Church it was 6.25pm and it took him five minutes to get to 29 Wolverton Street.

In his thoroughly researched book *The Killing of Julia Wallace*, Jonathan Goodman quotes, on the basis of the original and unabridged transcript, the cross-examination of Close by Roland Oliver. I include the comments of Goodman's, made no doubt on the basis of his enquiries, with persons conversant with the case, including Hector Munro, Wallace's solicitor who was, of course present at the trial:

"Just a little more detail about this" Roland Oliver said drily, as he rose to take up the questioning, and then proceeded to establish step by step, action by action, the boys movements from the time he passed Holy Trinity Church, until he left the doorstep of 29 Wolverton Street, having delivered the milk to Mrs Wallace.

After a dozen questions, each of them relating to a different action during the first half of the journey, Oliver broke off to ask in an astonished voice "Do you really say you did all this in five minutes?" "yes" the boy said "I have been over the ground with two detectives and it took me five minutes."

Shaking his head ever so slightly, Oliver went on to reconstruct the second half of the incident packed journey:

"You met Elsie Wright in Letchworth Street?"

"Yes"

"And if she says that the time was something like twenty to seven would you not agree with her, is that right?"

"No sir"

"Do you remember this – that as you stood on Mrs Wallace's doorstep was there a paper boy at the next house?"

"I do not remember"

Until now Close has seemed to be quite enjoying his spell in the witness box. But as Oliver turned to questions concerning the meeting with the other children on the night of the murder, the boy's manner changed abruptly. His voice became faltering; at times hardly audible; he fidgeted with his hands; his gaze flickered about the court, as if he were searching for someone who might come to his assistance. He looked very uncomfortable indeed.

"We have now got to the 21st" Oliver said "on the evening of the 21st did you have a conversation with Elsie Wright and was there also another boy there named Metcalf?"

"Yes"

"Did he ask you this: What time were you there?"

Before Oliver had completed the question Close was replying "I do not re-member"

"Just try and remember will you?" Oliver snapped "Perhaps this next thing will bring it back to your mind. Did you say At a quarter to seven?"

"No sir" Close said quickly

"Think. I suggest to you, in the presence of Kenneth Caird, Elsie Wright, and this boy Metcalfe, you said you were there at a quarter to seven"

"No" Close mumbled, "between half past six and a quarter to seven"

"Did you say that?"

A pause; and then in not much more than a whisper "I think so"

"You were there between half past six and a quarter to seven. That was true was it?"

"Yes"

"Why have you sworn today that you were there at half past six; when did you think that?"

Back to mumbling "Later on"

"But when"

"The following Sunday"

"Since you gave evidence before?"

"No, the following Sunday"

"No, the following Sunday" Mr Justice Wright interpassed. "That is what he says?"

"I cannot catch everything he says because he is so indistinct" Oliver explained.

"Yes. It is a difficulty to everybody"

Continuing the cross-examination, Oliver said "I must put it to you; that you, in the presence of those other children said it was a quarter to seven when you were at Mrs Wallace's. Now you think hard. Is not that right?"

Not just a pause this time but complete silence.

Eventually, leaning to his right and speaking in a grandfatherly tone, the judge broke the silence with: "What do you say about it?"

No reply, the boy shook his head slightly

"Do not shake your head" the judge said injecting a note of sharpness into his voice.

Still no reply.

So the judge gave up, leaning back in his seat he suggested; "Perhaps he is tired"

"Are you feeling alright?" Oliver asked the boy

At last: "Yes"

"Will you just apply your mind to what I put to you? Did you not say that you took the milk to Mrs Wallace at a quarter to seven?"

"No. Between half past six and a quarter to seven"

84

"It has taken you a long time to answer. You were not feeling ill were you?"

"No"

"He shook his head several times and could not bring himself to speak" the judge said to no one in particular.

"Do you remember" Oliver said still on the question of the quarter to seven, "the boy Metcalfe saying this to you; The police ought to know because in the papers it said Mr Wallace went out at a quarter past six, and if you saw her at a quarter to seven people could not think Wallace has done it?"

"No"

"Do you say you cannot remember or he did not say it?"

"I am sure he did not say it"

"Are you prepared to swear he did not say that?"

"No. He persuaded me to go to the police"

"Yes. But do not you remember the newspapers had said quite wrongly Mr Wallace went out at 6.15?" Oliver insisted.

"No"

"Are you sure then, that nothing at that sort was said?"

Another pause, another mumbled reply: "I cannot swear to it"

"That is quite honest" Oliver said "You may have forgotten"

His voice more relaxed now he went on: "Did you rather make a joke about it that evening when they wanted you to go to the police?"

"Do you remember you put your thumbs in your waist coat like that (illustrated) and said well I am the missing link?"

A pause

"Well did you?"

Close shook his head "No"

"Nothing like that?"

"No, Sir"

Oliver was speaking sharply again. "You have said they were present and persuaded you to go to the police. What I am putting to you is this – that you were rather reluctant to go to the police?"

"Well naturally" Close answered.

"And said you were the missing link?"

"No"

"You say you were reluctant to go" the judge asked.

"No"

Oliver did a double take "He said naturally he was reluctant"

"No, naturally I was not reluctant" Close said.

"If they were to say you used that expression, that is quite wrong is it?"

"Yes, Sir"

"It is a funny thing to invent, do you not think?"

Very funny Close thought. He sniggered "Yes" he said.

"Do not answer carelessly" Oliver thundered.

"Just think if during that evening you did not use that expression?"

Pouting now, Close muttered "No. Sir"

"Nobody is saying it is very wicked of you if you did, I am only trying to find out what you did say"

"Well I did not say it" Close cried, desperation lending defiance to the reply

"You swear you did not?" Oliver asked finally

"Yes, Sir"

Hemmerde rose to re-examine: 'Did you know that it was said in the papers that the prisoner left at 6.15?' he asked.

Twice during his cross-examination Close has sworn one thing, only to be pressed into saying another. Now he contradicted himself again by answering 'Yes'.

Doing his best to keep the surprise out of his voice Hemmerde said 'You knew that?'

'Yes' the boy persisted.

The poor performance of Alan Close was greatly accentuated by four other witnesses. These were Allison Wildman, Douglas Metcalfe, Kenneth Campbell Caird and David Jones. Mr Justice Wright criticised the Crown severely for failing to call two of these witnesses. In his summing up he said:

> I must say I do not agree with any attacks that were made upon the police in their conduct of this case. I think they have done their duty with great enthusiasm and ability, but I cannot help thinking that they were guilty of an error of judgement in not calling the two witnesses Jones and Wildman in the course of the prosecution. It is true that Jones's times may be a little uncertain, and Wildman, although he had mentioned it to his mother the next day, had already associated, although I do not think that ought to affect the position, with the solicitor for the defence. But that rather indicates in a case of this sort, where the ascertainment of the time within as narrow a limit as possible is so important, that they are witnesses who I think ought to have been put before the jury in the case by the prosecution. The case for the prosecution as it stood depended entirely on the evidence of the boy Close. If you think that the time was something like 6.35, then deducting 6.35 from even 6.50 or still less 6.47, you get a very narrow limit of time, for the prisoner, if it were the prisoner who did this, to do all that he must have done.

In the event it was the defence who called those witnesses. Douglas Metcalfe, a paper boy, said that about twenty or a quarter to seven he was near Wolverton Street. He had been told by someone this was the time. He then spent five minutes talking to some boys. He saw Wildman leaving Wolverton Street at that time. He further said that the day after the murder he heard Close say that he had seen Mrs Wallace alive at a quarter to seven. Cross-examined by Hemmerde he denied that Close had seen her between 6.30pm and 6.45pm. Close, he maintained, had said 'point blank' a quarter to seven.

Kenneth Campbell Caird stated in evidence that on the evening of January 21st he heard Allan Close say that he last saw Julia Wallace alive at a quarter to seven.

Allison Wildman said that she saw Close standing on the top step of 29 Wolverton Street at 27 minutes to seven and that he was still standing there when she went away.

The failure of the prosecution to call these young people was described by the judge as 'an error of judgement'. That expression looks a little generous. The police had their statements which they forwarded to the prosecution solicitor and hence to Edward Hemmerde. As counsel in charge of the Crown case the decision whether or not to produce them as witnesses was his. The fact that only Close was called on this vital point indicates that Hemmerde believed their evidence would seriously undermine the Crown case. A witness who is called by one side and then proceeds to contradict evidence already given on behalf of that side puts the counsel concerned in an embarrassing and difficult position. If his evidence is left to stand those who have given evidence before are badly compromised. If on the other hand counsel applied to treat him as a hostile witness the impression upon the jury can be well nigh disastrous. What kind of case is it where a barrister is obliged to attack his own witness? Hemmerde with his knowledge and experience in these matters, decided to leave the four young people out of the picture. This was a tactic which might have had a calamitous effect with the jury. In the event it did not.

Hemmerde continued his lengthy opening speech by describing Wallace's search for the non-existent Menlove Gardens East and what he viewed as his suspiciously frequent enquiries. Then he detailed the situation when Wallace returned to his house and discovered the body of his wife. Various adverse observations were made concerning the conduct of Wallace at the murder scene: His alleged pretence of being unable to gain entry at first to his house; the absence of any agony or grief at finding Julia's corpse; his strangely controlled manner throughout; his visiting the upstairs part of the premises on his first arrival; the fact of his mackintosh lying on one side of the body; the absence of the metal object which was used as a poker. All this said, it must be admitted by even those who have always been convinced of Wallace's guilt, that none of these things constituted any kind of direct evidence. Wallace's clothes had been examined and bore no traces of blood. This presented one of the greatest problems for the prosecution. With blood liberally spread about as a result of the ferocious onslaught it was inconceivable that the assailant could escape unmarked. Hemmerde met this obstacle head on:

> One of the most famous criminal trials was of a man who committed a crime when he was naked. A man might perfectly well commit a crime wearing a raincoat, as one might wear a dressing gown and come down, when he is just going to do this, with nothing on which blood could fasten and with anything like care, he might get away, leaving the raincoat there and go and perform the necessary washing if he was very careful.

This pronouncement which was a 'bombshell' in the course of the case clearly referred to the murder of Lord William Russell by Francois Benjamin Courvoisier in 1840. This was far from being a perfect analogy. It was never proved that Courvoisier was naked when he slit his master's throat. This, as was so much in the Wallace case, was a matter of supposition.

Hemmerde then gave an account of the signs of burglary in the premises and the reasons why the police and he suggested, the jury too, should come to the conclusion that there had been an attempt by the murderer to create the false impression that the intended crime has been theft and that Julia Wallace was killed in order to silence her.

Hemmerde read Wallace's statement made on the day of the murder. Having done so he made a particular point of the meeting on the 21 January between Wallace and Beattie. Wallace pressed Beattie for the time of the telephone call to the chess club, saying it was of great importance to him. He also made a comment to the effect that he had been with the police and that they had cleared him. When subsequently questioned about his conversation by Superintendent Moore, Wallace admitted that it had been indiscreet of him.

Hemmerde spoke confidently about Professor MacFall's evidence, but in fact the inadequate tests applied by MacFall to the body very much reduced the value of what he had to say.

Finally, Hemmerde came to his peroration:

I have had to open these facts at some length to you because you must know exactly what the story is, the burden that the Crown is attempting to prove in this case. If you think that the evidence laid before you leads irresistibly to the conclusion beyond all reasonable doubt, that this man, for some reason that we cannot define, killed his wife that night, you will have no hesitation in doing your duty. If on the other hand you say: In the absence of all motive we find there is, or think there is, some reasonable doubt, you will have no hesitation then in doing your duty. The case, as I say, is a difficult one and a painful one. All I can do is to set out to you the facts upon which we rely. The matter will be for you to determine, whether the evidence which the Crown lays before you really supports this charge of murder. This is not a case where you will be in any way concerned with other possible verdicts such as manslaughter. If this man did what he is charged with doing, it is murder, foul and unpardonable; few more brutal murders can ever have been committed – this elderly, lonely woman literally hacked to death for apparently no reason at all. Without an apparent enemy in the world, she goes to her account, and if you think the case is fairly proved against this man, that brutally and wantonly he sent this unfortunate woman to her account, it will be your duty to call him to his account.

It is unnecessary to repeat the evidence for the prosecution which we have already examined in detail. Suffice it to record Wallace's statement at the magistrates' court when asked if he wished to say anything in answer to the charge:

I plead not guilty to the charge made against me and I am advised to reserve my defence, I would like to say that my wife and I lived together on the very happiest terms during the period of some eighteen years of our married life. Our relations were those of complete confidence in, and affection for each other. The suggestion that I murdered my wife is monstrous; that I should attack and kill her is to all who know me, unthinkable, and the more so when it must be realised I could not gain one advantage by committing such a deed, nor do the police suggest that I gained any advantage. On the contrary, in actual fact I have lost a devoted and loving comrade, my home life is completely broken up and everything which I hold dear has been ruthlessly parted and torn from me. I am now to face the torture of this nerve wracking ordeal. I protest once more that I am entirely innocent of the terrible crime.

Hemmerde put in Wallace's statement and closed the case for the prosecution.

Roland Oliver now had the heavy responsibility of making two important decisions upon which the fate of his client might well depend. The first of these was: Should he submit to the judge that there was no case to go to the jury. The grounds for such a submission had to be either that there was no evidence or no sufficient evidence produced by the prosecution upon which a jury could properly convict or that such evidence as had been put before the court had been so discredited by other contrary testimony under cross-examination that the same principle applied. If the argument by defence counsel is successful the judge will direct the jury to enter a verdict of not guilty and the case is over. There is no mid-way verdict in England such as the Scottish 'not proven'. ('Not proven' is not the same as an acquittal. It amounts to a declaration that the evidence was insufficient, but it is not a clear statement that the defendant is innocent.) If, on the other hand, the ruling goes against the submission then the case proceeds. This does not put the defence at any disadvantage. In the event Oliver made no submission, and those who have regarded the Crown case as weak have criticised him for doing so. However, Oliver, one of the leading advocates of his day was aware of a danger. During argument between counsel on this point the jury leave court and are confined to their room. However, intelligent jury men and women will be aware of the nature of the discussion going on. If the ruling of the judge is that there is a *prima facie* case against the accused that fact may not make a good impression on the jury. Moreover, while it is true that as the prosecution stood there was no direct evidence of Wallace's involvement, Oliver would have been aware that the judge might take the view that the totality of the circumstantial evidence was sufficient to found a case. Finally, it would take a bold judge, in such a serious trial, to put an end to the proceedings at the half-way stage.

The second matter which it fell to Oliver to decide was an even more onerous responsibility. This was the question of whether or not to call his client to give evidence. Here again there are dangers attached to either course. If the defendant goes into the witness box and makes a bad impression on the court, either by reason of an unattractive personality or because he gives his evidence poorly or because he is badly shaken in cross-examination, his chances of acquittal will consequently be reduced. If on the other hand, he declines to go into the witness box the judge may, and probably, will make adverse comments on this in his summing-up, and the members of the jury will ask themselves what the defendant, if innocent, has to hide. A further consideration is the rule of procedure that deprives defending counsel of the last word with the jury if he calls evidence. Past, well-known cases illustrate the problems that can arise for the defence when one or other of these courses are taken.

In 1909 Oscar Slater, who was charged with the murder of Marion Gilchrist, was not allowed to speak in his own defence. He was convicted, but finally released on his retrial. In 1912 Frederick Seddon gave evidence, but although his answers were smooth and plausible they failed to convince the jury who returned a verdict of guilty. In 1912, Major Herbert Armstrong, accused of the murder of his wife was confident of acquittal. He went into the witness box but his defence collapsed under the cross-examination, unusually, of the judge, Mr Justice Derby, concerning small quantities of arsenic found on his person and in his office. In December 1922 Edith Thompson, charged together with Frederick Bywaters with the murder of her husband insisted, against the advice of her counsel, on entering the witness box and testifying on her own behalf. The very poor impression she made on the jury resulted in her conviction and subsequent execution. By way of contrast Dr John Bodkin Adams, who was charged with the murder of Edith Morrell, refrained from giving evidence and was acquitted, in the opinion of many, somewhat fortunately for him.

Both Hemmerde and Oliver knew perfectly well that the only evidence against Wallace was purely circumstantial. There was no direct evidence at all that Wallace was the killer of his wife. For this reason Hemmerde had seen it as his task to pile innuendo on suspicion, imputation upon imputation and then say to the jury: confronted with all this, and coupled with the fact that there is no other suspect, can you doubt that the case is proved against this accused person? Oliver for his part also saw his assignment with equal clarity to say to the jury: In a court of law suspicion added to presumption added to conjecture amount to nothing. Can you, by your verdict, deprive a man of his life on such slender grounds?

Roland Oliver rose to open the case for the defence. Unlike Hemmerde's 'tour de force' Oliver's address was much shorter, but a practical appeal to the common sense and reasonable view of the jury:

> Members of the jury, this case has been put to you like this: If the accused did not commit this murder who did? That is not the way to approach it. It should be asked, who is the man? You know something of Wallace now, He is fifty two, a delicate, mild man, liked by everyone who knew him; a man of considerable education, and refined, and as his diary shows, one with considerable gifts of expression. That is the man charged with this frightful crime, The question you will ask is why? There is no suggestion of ill-feeling between Wallace and his wife. He had £152 in the bank [at least £1,000 in today's money]. He had nothing to gain, and there was no suggestion of any other woman. If this man is to be convicted for a murder on the flimsiest circumstantial evidence, is it possible to say why?

Oliver then turned to deal with Professor MacFall's potentially damaging outburst regarding the mental state of the killer:

> It has been suggested that this crime was committed by someone in a state of frenzy. This suggestion was made because it was realised that this motive-less crime, alleged to have been committed by a devoted husband, presented almost insuperable problems. In fifty two years no one had ever suggested the accused was not perfectly sane. He has been under medical supervision

ever since his arrest and I ask you to disregard that suggestion. This was no sudden frenzy. If the accused did this thing, he calculated it all at least twenty four hours before, for the prosecution case stood or fell on the authenticity of the telephone call twenty four hours before. It could be proved that this perfectly normal man was behaving perfectly normally throughout January 19th and 20th which meant that, contemplating this frightful crime, he was going about his daily business and showing no signs of it! Let me say now, that this is what is sometimes called a police case. If there is one kind of crime that is an abomination to the police, it is an unsolved murder. Everybody attacks them if they cannot get a solution.

At this point having made a generous concession to the difficulties facing the police, Oliver attacks a piece of evidence which he saw as potentially damaging to his client:

Thus, because Constable Rothwell sees Wallace with his hands on his eyes, he was ghastly and wiping his eyes, thinking of course of the crime he was going to commit that evening! I can call as many witnesses as you want to hear, to say that on the day of the murder there was nothing wrong with Wallace at all.

In the event Oliver called three witnesses. This somewhat scornful view of Rothwell's evidence expressed by Oliver ignores several factors. First, a trained officer, who knew Wallace well, passed very close to him when making the observation; secondly, there is a great deal of difference between a man wiping his eyes because they are smarting and someone showing signs of acute distress; thirdly, although the murder had not as yet taken place there may have been some continuing situation between Wallace and his wife which caused the symptoms which the officer observed; and fourthly, Wallace, as seen earlier, was a man with a remarkable gift for subduing his emotions at short notice. The inference that the police are using a weak piece of evidence to bolster their case should also be noted.

Oliver then turned to the telephone call:

Where was the evidence to support the suggestion that Wallace sent the telephone message to himself? Three operators said that it was a perfectly ordinary man's voice, and Mr Beattie, who had known Wallace for well over eight years, said it would require a great stretch of imagination to think the voice was Wallace's. If he did not send that message he is an innocent man, and how can it be said that the prosecution have even started to prove it ...

For two hours he played chess with that message in his pocket, and won his game. What did they think must have been going on in his mind if that was his message and the stepping stone to the murder of his wife? What sort of chess would he play? It may occur to you that a man planning the murder would avoid telephoning Wallace when Wallace might himself answer the call. If he had watched Wallace walk away from his house on the 19th, why did he not go in then and do the murder?

A point here for the prosecution as much as for the defence. One reason against it was that the watcher could not be sure he had gone to the chess club. Another was that there would be more money in the house on the Tuesday evening. This assumes that the watcher knew where Wallace lived, the nature of his business and the size of the sum available in his house at this time – yet no suspect had been put before the jury – or indeed uncovered by the police in spite of all their endeavours to find one.

If Wallace had, as alleged by the police, been preparing an alibi, it would have been some preparation to say that his wife would have let in Qualtrough, or anyone else, had they called but, in actual fact he had said she should let no one in unless she had known them personally. He also said he could not think of anyone who knew he would be going to the club. These things spoke loudly against it being a concocted alibi (they also greatly narrowed the field against anyone other than Wallace himself being the killer).

Oliver then turned to the vexed question of the time factor:

The vital point in the case was: When was Mrs Wallace last seen alive? It was common ground that Wallace must have left the house within a minute of two of 6.45pm, if he left even at 7.30 he was almost certain to be innocent [this was impossible, since he was seen on the tram at 7.06 or 7.10] but if he left at any time after 6.30 he must be innocent. [We only have Wallace's uncorroborated evidence as to when he left home, if he left at 6.50 that leaves twenty minutes in which the murder could have been committed].

In considering what the murderer had to do between the crime and leaving the house, you must remember that Wallace was searched the same night, and there was no trace of blood on his clothes, hands, face or boots; yet according to witnesses he must have been heavily splattered with blood. Before he left he must be absolutely clean. His clothes could not be washed, but have to be got rid of. For the first time you now hear the suggestion that Wallace was naked in a mackintosh. If so his face, hair, hands and legs from the knees down would be covered in blood. He would have to have a bath and dress himself. There was no sign that anyone had had a bath at that time [This is surely the strongest point in Wallace's favour].

Oliver then mentioned the question of the weapon:

The bar mentioned in the case was not found in the only piece of waste ground on his way out that night, or in any drain, Where was it?

Then Oliver returned to the time issue:

It would take time to burn the mackintosh. If the witness Close was right, Wallace had from 6.30, or some time later, until about quarter to seven, but I shall call three witnesses against whom not a word can be said [Wildman,

Metcalfe and Cairns]. One of them said that Close stated afterwards that he had seen Mrs Wallace alive at a quarter to seven when he delivered the milk. When this came to the knowledge of the police it must have been a terrible shock, for if Close had delivered the milk at a quarter to seven, this man was clear. The argument of delivering the milk at 6.30 was that it would give sufficient time for the crime to have been committed. [In cross-examination, Close had said the time was between 6.30 and a quarter to seven. This was halfway between the truth and the police case.]

Oliver mentioned that there was nothing suspicious about Wallace acting on the message, since he hoped for a good recompense, nor was there anything strange about his conversation with the tramway men or about his search for Menlove Gardens East. His actions on his return to his house were not incriminating in any way, nor were the calmness he showed after the discovery of his wife's body. As to the burns on the mackintosh that allegedly occurred when Julia fell and burnt her skirt on the fire, Oliver concluded:

> I ask you to remember Wallace's undoubted affection for his wife, the utter absence of motive, his condition of comfort so far as money was concerned, his character – a gentle, kindly man of refined tastes, who could write that diary and congratulate himself on seventeen years of married life. That is the man you are asked to convict of murder, and that is the man to whom I am now going to ask you to listen. I need not have called him, his story has been told over and over again to the police. I should not think there ever was a case in which so many statements were taken.

Oliver then called his client and Wallace entered the witness box. Wallace looked pale and tense but also well under control. Oliver's task at that point was not especially difficult. His client was an intelligent man who should have no difficulty with giving his evidence with assurance and clarity. Wallace had already made several statements to the police with no substantial variation between any of them. There was no reason to doubt that he would do the same in court.

Wallace began his evidence by reciting the more formal and uncontroversial matters of his age, marriage, employment and financial situation. He said that relations with his wife had always been good and that he had no motive whatever for murdering her. He said that three weeks out of four, in the course of his work he would collect anything between £30 and £40, but that each fourth week it might be anything between say £80 and £100. Sometimes even more. On the Monday and Tuesday in question he had collected £14 out of which he had paid out something like £10/10 shillings in sickness benefit leaving some £4 in cash. This sum of £4 was placed in the cash box which was found to be empty when the house was searched by the police. Other money which Wallace and his wife had saved was kept in a jar in the bedroom. This had been found when the house was searched. One note was smeared with blood.

Oliver then turned to the chess club and the mystery telephone call:

OLIVER: On January 19th had you any kind of quarrel with your wife, or at any time?

WALLACE: No, none whatever.

OLIVER: We know you were due to go and play a match of chess. I will take this as shortly as I can. What time did you leave your house to go to the chess club?

WALLACE: As near as I can tell you, about a quarter past seven.

Wallace's was the only evidence of this.

OLIVER: That is the time you gave to the police near the event?

WALLACE: Yes.

OLIVER: How did you go there, by what method? I do not want the whole route, but did you walk, or go by train or how?

WALLACE: I walked up Richmond Park, turned the corner by the church and up Belmont Road, and there caught a tram.

This was not the quickest route, but one which brought him within easy reach of the telephone box.

OLIVER: It has been suggested that you used the telephone box to telephone a message to yourself. Is there a word of truth in that?

WALLACE: Absolutely none.

OLIVER: You have heard the evidence given by Mr Beattie as to what happened at the chess club?

WALLACE: Yes.

OLIVER: Is that substantially correct.

WALLACE: It is.

OLIVER: Were you engaged in your game when he spoke to you?

WALLACE: I was.

OLIVER: I think you were due to play a man named Mr Chandler, but he was not there, and you played a back match. Is that so?

WALLACE: Yes that is so.

OLIVER: With a Mr McCartney?

WALLACE: Yes.

OLIVER: You made a note of the name and address in your book which is here?

WALLACE: Yes.

OLIVER: Was that a little memorandum book? It does not seem to be much used, but there are a few entries in it.

WALLACE: It is a new one, sent down by our company at the beginning of the year, and has not many entries in it except one or two addresses.

OLIVER: This is where you put it?

WALLACE: Yes.

OLIVER: Did you understand that there was a possibility of business from the message?

WALLACE: Yes, I understood it so.

OLIVER: What sort of policy might you expect a father to give a son who has just come of age? What type of policy do you get for that, an endowment policy or a life policy?

WALLACE: Seeing the name and the daughter coming of age had been suggested, I considered it might result in a policy of something like £100 endowment, or something of that nature. I did not expect it would be less than that.

OLIVER: We have been told you would get twenty percent of the first payment?

WALLACE: Yes.

OLIVER: You went on with your game. Do you remember when it finished?

WALLACE: No. I do not.

OLIVER: We have been told you got there at a quarter to eight?

WALLACE: Yes.

OLIVER: Did you go home soon after your game finished, do you remember or did you wait?

WALLACE: I cannot say exactly. I think the game was finished a little before closing time, and I would probably look on some other game that was being played.

OLIVER: Was it a little before ten?

WALLACE: About ten.

OLIVER: That would be a fairly long game, over two hours?

WALLACE: Yes.

OLIVER: And you walked back with Mr Caird?

WALLACE: Yes. To the car.

Oliver then came to the day of the murder. Wallace described how he had been collecting all day before returning home to his wife a little after 6pm. Oliver then came to the evidence of PC Rothwell:

OLIVER: Were you your usual self that afternoon?

WALLACE: Quite.

OLIVER: It has been suggested by a policeman that as he bicycled past you, at about half past three, you had a ghastly appearance, and were wiping your eyes with your sleeve?

WALLACE: I heard the suggestion.

OLIVER: Is it true?

WALLACE: No. It is not.

OLIVER: I mean that it was through any distress?

WALLACE: No; certainly not.

OLIVER: Do your eyes ever water in January?

WALLACE: They may do yes.

OLIVER: If they did what would you do?

WALLACE: Probably take out my handkerchief and insert it under my glasses and just wipe them.

Oliver then turned to the day of the murder. Wallace repeated much the same as he had said in his previous statements: He had arrived home shortly after six, taken tea with his wife and then after getting a number of forms ready he had gone upstairs and washed his hands and face. After this he changed his collar and brushed his hair. He then left the house by the back door. Julia accompanied him as far as the back yard door where he instructed her to bolt the door after her. He did not hear her bolt it. (This last item differs from what he had told PC Williams, according to that officer. Why could he have got that wrong? Was it because by that time Julia was dead and could not have accompanied him anywhere?) He said when he left her she was perfectly well.

Asked about the search for Menlove Gardens East Wallace repeated the account he had already given to the police. He maintained that he spoke to nobody on his way home and that the evidence given by Lily Hall was not true. He did not know her at all, although she might know him by sight.

Oliver then took his client through the events on his arrival at home: the difficulties with the back and front doors; his meeting with the Johnston's; his entry into his house and the fact that he agreed substantially with the accounts which they had given. He confirmed that his wife knew all about the telephone call and that he had conferred with her before deciding to go. Wallace, questioned by Oliver, described the layout of the house and the use to which the front parlour was put. Oliver then asked him about the discovery of his wife's body, the missing iron bar and the fact of his mackintosh being found in a blood stained condition partly wrapped around the body:

OLIVER: What did you call?

WALLACE: I shouted out my wife's name twice Julia, Julia. I probably also said are you there? But I do not remember that.

OLIVER: Was there a light in her bedroom?

WALLACE: Yes.

OLIVER: Up or down?

WALLACE: Down.

OLIVER: Did you turn it up?

WALLACE: Yes.

OLIVER: We have been told your progress could be traced looking into the other two rooms on that floor?

WALLACE: Yes.

OLIVER: It is said that the bed in the front bedroom was somehow disarranged, and there were some of your wife's hats on it?

WALLACE: Yes.

OLIVER: Do you know anything at all about that?

WALLACE: I do not think I had been in that room for probably a fortnight before the twentieth or nineteenth of January.

OLIVER: Had that anything to do with you?

WALLACE: Nothing at all.

OLIVER: You then came down. You had been in the kitchen and the back kitchen, and the only room left was the front parlour?

WALLACE: Yes.

OLIVER: Was there any light in that?

WALLACE: No.

OLIVER: As you went into it, did you do anything with regard to lighting it, and if so, tell us exactly what you did?

WALLACE: When I came downstairs and approached the front-room door, it was closed, but not latched, that is to say it was simply pulled to.

OLIVER: Had you any matches with you?

WALLACE: I had a box in my hand that I had used upstairs.

OLIVER: You told us you lit the middle kitchen gas, and had the box in your hand?

WALLACE: Yes.

OLIVER: What did you do?

WALLACE: The door was closed to, and I pushed it open a little, and then I struck a match in quite the ordinary way, that I probably did every night. I went into the room in the dark. I held it up, and as I held it up I could see my wife was lying there on the floor.

OLIVER: You told the officer you thought she was in a fit?

WALLACE: That was my first impression, but it only lasted possibly a fraction of a second, because I stooped down, with the same match, and I could see there was evidence of signs of disturbance and blood, and I saw she had been hit.

OLIVER: Did you light the light?

WALLACE: Yes, I did.

OLIVER: Which light?

WALLACE: The one on the right hand side near the window.

OLIVER: Why did you light that one?

WALLACE: It is the one we always use.

OLIVER: That and the tap of the gas stove are on the same side?

WALLACE: Yes.

OLIVER: When you saw your wife lying there, I suppose it follows you avoided treading on her as you went past?

WALLACE: Certainly.

OLIVER: When you got the light on, tell us, in your own way, what you did.

WALLACE: The moment I got the gas lit I turned round of course, examined my wife, and I got hold of her left hand, that was lying over her body, and felt the pulse, and could not find any appearance of life at all, and I looked into her face and I saw then she was obviously quite dead. Well, I can hardly remember what I did then, but I know I came out of the house and rushed down the yard and informed my neighbours, and asked them to come in.

OLIVER: We have the story from that point. With regard to the weapon which has been suggested. Do you know anything about a piece of iron which was said to be against the gas stove, used for cleaning under it?

WALLACE: I do not know anything about it at all.

OLIVER: Have you ever seen it?

WALLACE: No.

OLIVER: It is said to have been propped against the gas stove, and some times close up to the kerb?

WALLACE: I have never seen the piece of iron.

OLIVER: You have not?

WALLACE: No.

OLIVER: I suppose the cleaning of the house had not very much to do with you, had it?

WALLACE: No. Not very much.

Oliver then turned to the much debated subject of Wallace's demeanour, which the prosecution maintained was one of unnatural, almost callous indifference. Questioned by Oliver in this matter, Wallace replied:

WALLACE: Well, I remember that I was extremely agitated, and that I was trying to keep as calm and as cool as possible. Probably I was smoking cigarettes for something to do; I mean to say the reaction was something more than I could stand. I had to do something to avoid breaking down. I did sit down in a chair on one or two occasions, and I do remember I did break down absolutely; I could not help it or avoid it. I tried to be as calm and as cool as possible.

OLIVER: Is there anyone in the world who could take the place of your wife in your life?

WALLACE: No. There is not.

OLIVER: Or to live for?

WALLACE: No.

OLIVER: And no children?

WALLACE: No.

Questioned about the mackintosh Wallace agreed with the evidence given about his words and actions by Mrs Johnston and PC Williams.

On the crucial issue of whether Julia would have admitted anyone to the house in his absence Wallace said:

WALLACE: The questions were put to me [by Inspector Gold] in such a way that I felt I had to give the names of people. It was put to me something like this: As far as you can remember, would your wife admit anybody to the house? and I gave him the names of a number of people that my wife would know and admit at night.

OLIVER: Had you at that time considered the possibility of a man coming and giving the name Qualtrough to your wife? Looking at it now, if someone did come and give the name of Qualtrough on that night, do you think she would have let him in?

WALLACE: Seeing I had gone to meet a Mr Qualtrough, I think she would, because she knew all about the business [why should Qualtrough pay a visit when he would have expected Wallace to call on him at his house in Menlove Gardens East in under an hours time?]

OLIVER: It is only a matter of speculation?

WALLACE: Yes.

OLIVER: If she had let him in, where would she have taken him?

WALLACE: Into the front room. There is no question about that.

Wallace then explained why he had said, in his conversation with Beattie, that the time of the phone call was important to him. This he said was because if he left home at about a quarter past seven, and the call was made at seven, it would mean he would be completely in the clear. (There was no corroboration for the time Wallace said he left the house.) He said he realised he had been followed and was therefore under suspicion. Consequently, he now knew it was indiscreet to speak to Mr Beattie, a potential witness in the case.

When Edward Hemmerde rose to cross-examine tension rose in court. Notwithstanding his confident and combative manner Hemmerde must have realised that his task was no easy one. There was so little on which Wallace could be driven into a corner; virtually nothing on which he could conclusively be shown up as a liar. All was a matter of supposition and interpretation. Moreover the subject of his attack was a shrewd man fighting for his life. Hemmerde began by going straight away to the night of the murder. He questioned Wallace on the state of the parlour when the body was found, the implication being that he had said nothing to Julia, before he murdered her, about the visit to 'Qualtrough'.

HEMMERDE: So far as the use of your parlour is concerned, did you use it much for music?

WALLACE: Yes, quite a fair amount.

HEMMERDE: When you had an off evening, I suppose, being both musical, you were inclined to spend it with music?

WALLACE: Yes.

HEMMERDE: And I suppose being, to some extent a musician, you did not leave your piano open when you were not using it?

WALLACE: Yes, we did.

HEMMERDE: Always?

WALLACE: Yes. Pretty nearly always.

HEMMERDE: One sees it in the photograph taken after the murder?

WALLACE: Yes.

HEMMERDE: And one sees music upon it?

WALLACE: Quite possible.

HEMMERDE: Have you the book of photographs there?

WALLACE: No. That is a plan.

HEMMERDE: Just take it. Can your knowledge of music tell me what was on the piano?

WALLACE: No, it cannot, except it might be two pieces of music.

HEMMERDE: Yes, it might be two pieces of music, it might be the viola score and the other.

WALLACE: I think it is too long to be violin music.

HEMMERDE: You think it is. When you used the piano for music on a night in January, you would naturally have the fire lighted?

WALLACE: Yes, we did.

HEMMERDE: And the gas?

WALLACE: And the gas.

HEMMERDE: Had you any other light to throw upon the music other than the gas?

WALLACE: We had the two gas-jets, no other.

HEMMERDE: Two?

WALLACE: Yes.

HEMMERDE: And you generally use them both I suppose?

WALLACE: No if we were by ourselves we would use one.

HEMMERDE: For the music?

WALLACE: Yes.

HEMMERDE: Then if you had been going that night to stay at home, it would have been quite natural that the piano should be open, and the fire lit, and you would be having your ordinary musical evening, if you had not had your appointment with Qualtrough?

WALLACE: No. Probably we should not have had any music that evening. Her cold would have made her say it will be rather cold in the front room. I do not think we will bother tonight with music.

HEMMERDE: She might?

WALLACE: Yes.

HEMMERDE: Her cold had not been too bad to walk out into the yard and see you out?

WALLACE: That is so.

HEMMERDE: She was wearing your mackintosh at the time?

WALLACE: No.

HEMMERDE: Her cold was evidently not at all bad?

WALLACE: We did not consider it serious.

HEMMERDE: And she was not a singer?

WALLACE: She had been at one time.

HEMMERDE: It was piano playing in which she was interested, and therefore the cold would not affect her?

WALLACE: Not a bit.

HEMMERDE: Therefore, if you had made up your mind to stay at home, and she knew it, it would be perfectly natural that you would be spending your time there with the fire lit, gas lit, and playing music?

WALLACE: It would be quite natural.

HEMMERDE: Had you ever told your wife you were going out that night?

WALLACE: Certainly, we discussed it.

HEMMERDE: You discussed it?

WALLACE: We discussed it at teatime.

HEMMERDE: If your wife had not known you were going out that night, she might have got the room ready for you for the music?

WALLACE: Not unless I had asked her to do so.

HEMMERDE: No. But if you had asked her to do so?

WALLACE: She would have done it.

HEMMERDE: If you had let your wife know you were going to be in, that is just how the room might have been?

WALLACE: If we had decided to have music that is how the room might have been, naturally.

Hemmerde then questioned Wallace about his knowledge of the Menlove Gardens area, suggesting that it was much better than Wallace had admitted. Wallace agreed that in the past he had visited that district with his wife on several occasions and that he had attended the house of his superior, Mr Crewe, for the purpose of violin lessons. Crewe lived in Green Lane which joins Allerton Road and Menlove Avenue. Wallace said he had been to the home of Crewe that night but nobody was in. It was put to him, and Oliver conceded this, that he had not said any of this in his statements to the police. A telephone call to Crewe would have saved Wallace the trouble of the fruitless search for Menlove Gardens East.

Wallace agreed that no one knew he was going to be at the chess club on the Monday evening, or that he had told anybody that he would be there. Wallace was far too astute to be shifted from the account he had given to the police on several occasions and now repeated in court, except on very minor points. Consequently, Hemmerde devoted his cross-examination to exposing the absurdity of the whole Qualtrough story:

HEMMERDE: Anyone knowing the nature of the business, would know you when your monthly collections would be?

WALLACE: Any outside person would not know, certainly.

HEMMERDE: No, but anyone who knew sufficiently the methods of your business would know that as well?

WALLACE: They might do.

HEMMERDE: And if he was going to make a raid on your house and attack your wife alive, he would naturally choose the time of the monthly collection?

WALLACE: He might.

Now Hemmerde was making real progress, and Wallace is prevaricating. In the telephone call Qualtrough made it plan that he knew Wallace's business. Why therefore should he plan to steal from the house and kill Julia on a day, a Tuesday, when only a small sum of money would be in the house?

HEMMERDE: That would strike you as being the more natural, would it not? So far as you know had your wife got any enemies at all?

WALLACE: None, whatever.

HEMMERDE: As far as you know she had no enemies at all?

WALLACE: I do not think she had a single one.

HEMMERDE: And although you gave certain names to the police of persons she might have admitted, is there one of them against whom you have the slightest suspicion of having committed this offence?

WALLACE: No.

Hemmerde came back to the telephone call:

HEMMERDE: When Mr Qualtrough rang up on Monday night, we know he was a few hundred yards from your house?

WALLACE: I do not know.

HEMMERDE: You have heard he was at the call-box?

WALLACE: He was supposed to be there. I do not know.

HEMMERDE: You do not dispute that the café was rung up from there?

WALLACE: In the face of the evidence I cannot dispute that.

HEMMERDE: Very well then, you can say yes. He was about four hundred yards from your house. Your wife was alone, presumably he rang up the City Café, he must have expected you to be there?

WALLACE: One must presume that.

These answers appear to show that Wallace was stalling. He seems to be on the defensive. Like a cat with a mouse, Hemmerde pressed on with his attack on the Qualtrough story.

HEMMERDE: And of course Mr Qualtrough had no possible means of knowing whether you would receive it [the message] that night, because no one knew you were going to be at the club?

WALLACE: That is so.

HEMMERDE: Then he rang you up at 7.15 or 7.20, and without knowing you would ever get the message, and without knowing you would ever go to Menlove Gardens East, apparently he was ready waiting for your departure the next night?

WALLACE: It would look like it.

HEMMERDE: Did it ever occur to you that he would have to watch both doors, back and front?

WALLACE: No. It did not.

HEMMERDE: You are a man of business instincts, you could hardly be a Prudential agent if you were not?

WALLACE: That is so.

HEMMERDE: And you never had a message sent you before?

WALLACE: I have not.

HEMMERDE: You must have realised he had not the slightest idea as to whether he got your message or not, because you say no one knew you were going to be there?

WALLACE: Yes.

HEMMERDE: And therefore he never knew you were going to get his message, and in spite of that you go off to Menlove Gardens East?

WALLACE: Yes.

HEMMERDE: Not only could he not know that you would go, but he could not have known that you would look up a directory and find there was no such place?

WALLACE: No.

HEMMERDE: He would have to risk all that?

WALLACE: Yes.

HEMMERDE: And, of course, you could have found out at once, if you had looked up in the directory where Menlove Gardens East was or not?

WALLACE: I could have done.

HEMMERDE: And I suppose the slightest enquiry at the Prudential Office would have told you the town of Liverpool is divided into blocks, each under an agent. It would have been the simplest thing in the world to find out through the machinery at the hands of the Prudential whether there was such a place?

WALLACE: It was not necessary [arguably a strange reply].

Hemmerde then questioned Wallace about the various enquiries he made of the tram officials and other people, and concluded with the key words:

HEMMERDE: As a matter of fact, does it not strike you, looking back upon it now, that all these enquires were absolutely unnecessary; one simple enquiry of the policeman on point duty would have done it?

WALLACE: No, it does not strike me as being at all out of the way.

HEMMERDE: Where is Mr Crewe generally during the day?

WALLACE: At his office.

HEMMERDE: And that is on the telephone?

WALLACE: The office is on the telephone.

HEMMERDE: You only had to ring up Mr Crewe and find out where Menlove Gardens East was, and if it was near him?

WALLACE: I could have done but I did not think of it [a somewhat weak reply].

Wallace agreed that a false address would be necessary to the creation of an alibi, since it was a way to gather witnesses for that kind of defence.

Hemmerde put the crux of his cross-examination to Wallace:

HEMMERDE: Does not the whole thing strike you as very remarkable, that a man who does not know you should ring you up for business in another district, and expect you to go there, and yet, without knowing you had gone there or not, came and waited outside your house for the chance of murdering your wife?

WALLACE: Yes.

Hemmerde then put a number of questions to Wallace regarding the events on his arrival home; the missing iron bar; the locks on the doors and the mackintosh. But in these matters Wallace stood his ground and never appeared to be in serious difficulty.

Oliver re-examined his client and then called his further witnesses, Professor Dibble and Dr Coope, to point out the inadequate tests applied by Professor MacFall and Wildman, Metcalfe, Caird and Jones to qualify the evidence of Close and to reduce the period of time available for Wallace to commit the murder.

That concluded the evidence in the case. Final speeches and the judge's summing up now remained. Roland Oliver had called evidence and therefore, by the rules of procedure, had lost the right of having the last word with the jury. The early part of his speech, which is here quoted verbatim from the transcript of the trial, was a powerful plea which concentrated on three matters which told in favour of his client. Later on his address seems to have acquired a defensive character and in his final appeal he makes what by common consent was a very grave error indeed and nearly cost his client his life. The three points he made initially were: The evidence that the voice on the telephone was nothing like Wallace's; the time factor which showed Wallace did not have the time to commit the murder and carry out the consequent arrangements; and the absence of any sign of blood on Wallace. These arguments he put convincingly to the jury. With regard to other matters such as the burned mackintosh, the general demeanour of Wallace on finding his wife murdered, the missing iron bar, the questions about the doors and the lights at 28 Wolverton Street and the whole Qualtrough scenario he contented himself with his submission that there was nothing in any of these things which in common sense and reasonableness could be construed against Wallace.

Finally he came to the concluding part of his speech to the jury:

Members of the jury, I have finished. The onus in this matter, the burden of proof, is wholly upon the Crown. You have got a crime here without a motive; you have got a man here against whose character there is not a word

106

to be said; you have got a man here whose affection for his wife cannot be doubted. You are trying a man for the murder of a woman, who was his only companion, for no benefit. The Romans had a maxim which is as true today as it was then: no one ever suddenly became the basest of men. How can you conceive such a man with these antecedents doing such a thing as this. Finally, if I may say so, it is not enough that you should think it is possible that he did this – not merely enough, but it is not nearly enough

It was then that Oliver made the most extraordinary concession:

On looking at the two stories, you may say "Well, the story of the defence does not sound very likely, but the story of the prosecution does not sound very likely either"; and if that be the state of your minds then he is entitled to be acquitted. I suggest that this should be the state of your minds. The story for the defence is not very likely, but at least it is consistent with all the facts; the story for the prosecution sounds impossible.

It is inexplicable that such an experienced and distinguished barrister as Roland Oliver could have described his client's case as 'not very likely'. The words 'but at least it is consistent with all the facts' amount almost to an apology for the theory which the defence have urged upon the jury as an alternative to the prosecution case.

Hemmerde began his long address with a reminder of the duty of the Crown to prove the case beyond all reasonable doubt:

May it please your lordship, members of the jury. It now becomes my duty to address you finally on behalf of the prosecution. My learned friend need have no doubt. I shall not ask you to wait until my Lord addresses you before you learn, that if you are dissatisfied with the story of the prosecution and the story for the defence, the prosecution have failed to make out their case. I do not think any of you, could readily have been in doubt after you heard it that, in accordance with what I regard as my duty, I put before you that the burden of proof was on the prosecution and that you could not convict this man merely upon coincidences.

Hemmerde, in the course of a forceful speech, emphasised the various points to which he had adhered in presenting the Crown case. Let us therefore concern ourselves only with that part of his final discourse which deals with the telephone call so inextricably linked to the end of Julia Wallace's life:

Now I take my learned friends two points. Who sent the telephone message? is the first vital point; and what time have the prosecution established that Mrs Wallace was killed?, is the second vital point. Let us take the facts of the first. The prisoner admits that on the Monday night about 7.15 he left his house. About 7.15 obviously may mean two or three minutes one way or the other. He gave that statement early on – I think the night of the murder – and that statement is not and cannot be varied. The telephone box is four hundred yards from his house, walking five miles an hour, he would do that in rather under three minutes; walking four miles an hour, in rather over. He is a tall man, and one could probably fairly give him a good four miles an hour walking at night at 7.15. From the telephone box, about three minutes from his house, someone tries to get through to the City Café. My learned friend said how did the Recorder get the fact that nobody knew or could know he was going to be there? He must have got it from the police I did not, I got it from his client. In the deposition, as I put it to him, Inspector Gold, giving his evidence before the magistrates, and here again, said I asked him if he knew anyone who knew he was going to the club; and had he told anyone he was going? To that Wallace said No, I had not told anyone I was going and I cannot think of anyone who knew I was going; and upon that I based the statement that nobody would know that he was going or could know [a bad slip here on the part of Oliver]. It is suggested somebody might have looked at the match list up in the City Café, and I think you know, from Mr Beattie, that that was only provisional as people might never turn up for their matches.

Assuming he left the house on his three minute journey at 7.15 he could easily have been in that telephone box at 7.18; but by a singular coincidence the man who wanted him, Qualtrough, was in that telephone box at the identical time at which Mr Wallace might have been there, and, by another singular coincidence, at that moment was trying to ring up Mr Wallace. That is how it starts. The man in the box ringing up at a time when, on Mr Wallace's own time, he might perfectly well have been there, and it was a box that he had used, and it was the only box as my learned friend frankly admitted, anyone on such an occasion as this would be likely to use, because the other one was in a public library or in a shop, and naturally a man doing a thing like this would not want to go to a box where he would be observed. We know, whoever he was, he went to a box where there was no light, except an indirect light, and where anybody could perfectly well telephone without drawing any attention.

The man in the box telephoned through to the City Café. Nobody but Wallace knew that Wallace was going to be at the café; no one. That is his own story. The man rings up. Assuming for a moment that it was the prisoner, you can hardly imagine that he would ring up when he could speak to any member of the club without, to some extent, disguising his voice. You may think it difficult to disguise the voice. Some of you may have tried it before now and think it is pretty easy. That is entirely a matter for you. The voice on the telephone was confident and strong, but inclined to be gruff. If a person was imitating another person's voice, you might imagine he might do so in a voice which would have all those characteristics. That is what is suggested: That the man who rang up there was the prisoner and that he rang up no doubt disguising his voice. Now assuming that it was not the prisoner; a man whose name Wallace had never heard, a man who could not possibly know that Wallace would be at that place, because Wallace had told no body, rings up the club, and leaves a message of an appointment for the next night at Menlove Gardens East with a stranger. The stranger cannot tell him whether

Wallace is coming or not, but if he comes, he will give him the message. He is asked if he will not ring up later, he says no he has got some function on, some twenty-first birthday party. If it was Wallace, he obviously would say he could not ring up later, because he would not be there. If the man had important business, and he wanted to speak to a man he did not know, do you not think he would then want to ring up later? And remember, when he was ringing up, he was four hundred yards only from the house of Mr Wallace, and it is perfectly clear that he did not call there, and he did not leave any note there. What he did do, was to telephone up to a place where he could not know he was going to be. It is common ground that the man who rang up there, whether Wallace or another man, was planning the murder of the next night, therefore you would have thought he would be certain to see that his message was one which would get home to the person whose whereabouts he wanted to affect the next night. He does nothing of the sort. He leaves it with Mr Beattie, who cannot even tell him that Wallace is coming. He never enquires afterwards whether Wallace came there and got his message, but he leaves the whole thing there in the air. Can you believe that any man planning a crime the next night would not first of all see definitely that the man would be safely out of the way? What was there to prevent him sending a message to ask him to speak at a later time on the telephone? (It might be argued the other way that a man who contemplated murder would not want to use the telephone more than once if it could be avoided). Supposing it was Qualtrough himself on the telephone, he could say: I will ring up in an hour and see if he is there, and if was not there, well and good, But can you believe that the man would leave it just to chance as to whether he got that message or not? That is where we start.

Thus having demolished, at least to his own satisfaction, the defence theory about the telephone call, Hemmerde continued in the rest of his address to the jury, apart from some issues, to press home the main points which were prejudicial to Wallace.

And so the trial reached its final stage: The judge's summing up.

Those present at the trial and subsequent writers on the subject are agreed on one thing. Mr Justice Wright, in the clearest possible terms, within his duty to assist and not persuade the jury, summed up for an acquittal. This author recalls from his days at the Bar many judge's who summed up the cases before them in a variety of ways. They invariably performed their duty by emphasising to the jury that while the judges direction on law must be followed, the facts of the case were for them. However there were some judges who seemed unable to avoid disclosing the opinion which they themselves had formed. One judge is recalled whose summing up was frequently so antagonistic to the defence that it resembled a third speech for the prosecution. Mr Justice Wright's summation was the acme of fairness.

Wright began by dismissing any question of insanity:

As you all know, the crime of murder means the premeditated and deliberate and wrongful and felonious killing of another person. There can be no doubt at all here, that this poor woman was done to death by, first, a very crushing blow, and then, if she was not already dead, by a succession of ten other blows. It is not uncommon in the annals of crime that the murderer, having struck one blow, in some sort of insensate frenzy goes on to strike other blows. It does not follow merely from that that there can be any suggestion that the murderer was insane. In this case there is no question of insanity to be considered; it could only be raised by the defence, and it obviously was not raised, and could not be raised in the present matter, because it is perfectly clear that whoever murdered this woman did so in pursuance of a plan made the day before and commencing with the telephone message. Members of the jury, you, I believe, are living more or less in this neighbourhood; I come here as a stranger and knew nothing about the case until I came into court or looked at the depositions, and I need not warn you that you must approach this matter without any preconceived notions at all.

The judge then gave a careful direction to the jury as to their duty:

Your business here is to listen to the evidence, and to consider the evidence and nothing else. You are not even entitled to act, in fact you would not act, upon the speeches of counsel, either in the opening speech or any other speech, and any statement made which is not born out by the evidence, you will disregard any such statement, and, as I have said before, you will come with an open and unprejudiced mind to consider all this evidence given in great detail and more or less difficult to put together, which has been put before you.

Mr Justice Wright then pointed out to the jury the complete absence of direct evidence:

This murder, I should imagine, must be almost unexampled in the annals of crime. Here you have a murder committed some time on an evening in January. Committed in a populous neighbourhood in a house, and you have that murder so devised and so arranged that nothing remains which would point to anyone as the murderer; no signs of anyone having come into the house forcibly, no fingerprints, no marks of blood anywhere in the house – I mean apart from the marks due to the actual commission of the crime round the woman's head as she lay there – and no marks in the house. I disregard the little smear upon the note, which I will say something about later, but even that is not a fingerprint, it is a mere smear, and no weapon can be traced anywhere and, so far as can be ascertained, no conceivable motive in any human being, It is a most remarkable murder, but there it is. There is certainly no eye-witness except the actual murderer, besides the dead woman, and therefore the evidence in this case, and the evidence that can be brought against anybody here is purely circumstantial.

Mr Justice Wright then directed the jury on the matter of the circumstantial evidence. (I shall deal with this subject in the next chapter.) Sufficient to say here that his direction remains a model of judicial excellence for posterity.

The judge then instructed the jury on the separate functions of the Bench and the jury in a criminal trial:

> You have heard at very considerable length the evidence in this case, and you have had very forcible speeches from counsel on both sides, and they have put before you in very great detail their view of the evidence in the case. I am not saying that either of these speeches have been, or any of the speeches have been given at undue length, but the considerations have been fully laid before you. You are the judges of the facts; I am not the judge of the facts at all. But it is regular and usual, especially in these cases, for the judge to make some survey of the evidence which has been laid before the jury in the case, because it may help the jury, although they are the judges of fact. Of course, you will remember that you have heard the evidence, and you are the judges of the evidence, and if I omit or over stress any matter contrary to your view, it is your view which is the dominant view in this case.

Mr Justice Wright then turned to the complete absence of any motive:

> Now when it comes to consider the evidence here on the question of motive, I do not think I can say anything at all. All the evidence is that the prisoner and his wife, to all appearances were living together in happiness and in amity. You have heard the evidence. There was no pecuniary inducement that one can see for the prisoner to desire the death of his wife: She had a small insurance policy on her life, a matter of £20, and she had something like £90 in the savings bank. But there is no reason to think that he wanted that £20, for, if he did want it, he could have got it because he had a bank balance of his own. There was nothing that he could gain, so far as one can see, by her death. It can also be pointed out that there is no one else, as far as can be seen, who had anything to gain by her death if you exclude the hypothesis of the unknown robber, who, it is suggested, and it is a suggestion you will have to consider very carefully, may have committed this crime [This is a possibility that Hemmerde swept aside]. As I said before it is not a question of determining who or what sort of person other than the prisoner did the crime, or could have done the crime; it is a question whether it is brought home to the prisoner, and whether it is brought home to him by the evidence with such certainty as is required in a case of this sort. As far as the question of motive is concerned, you will form your own view about it, but as far as the prisoner is concerned there is no apparent motive.

On the subject of the telephone call the judge emphasised that here again the evidence was no more than circumstantial:

> Then there was the message sent on the telephone to the chess club. Now, whoever sent that message, of course must have known a great deal about

the prisoner's habits. It was said at one stage that no one could have known that he was going to the club that night. It may be that nobody could have known with certainty, but we know now that a notice appeared fixing the time at which members of the club will play, and that on this notice it appeared that the prisoner would be playing that night. So it is not a case in which the knowledge of the prisoner being at that club can be said with absolute certainty to be limited to him [a concession to the defence]. If there had been no probability of his going to the club that night at about that time, it might be that there would be a very strong presumption that it was the prisoner who went there. But it seems to me, although it is a matter entirely for you, that there must be on the evidence some possibility that someone else knew of the prisoner's possible movements, prospective movements, with sufficient confidence to take some action upon them [thereby suggesting to the jury there was a reasonable doubt].

It is said by the prosecution that it is difficult to conceive anybody doing such a thing, Various improbabilities are pointed out; How would they know when the prisoner was going to the café, how would they know that he had been to the café, why did they not ring up again? And all those sorts of things. Of course, if there were some other outside planning, with ingenious cunning, the purpose which he carried out to the last, for a motive which no one can understand and is apparently undiscoverable, it might be material for consideration; but you have got to ask yourselves: What is the reasonably certain evidence substantially excluding other possibilities to such an extent that you can find the fact established to your reasonable satisfaction, that it was the prisoner who rang up that night.

On the subject of the voice of the man calling himself, Qualtrough, the judge pointed out that Beattie, who had quite a long discussion with him and who knew the voice of Wallace well, said that by no stretch of the imagination could he associate the voice he heard with Wallace. Further, it was difficult to imagine that even if the voice was disguised Mr Beattie would not recognise it as that of Wallace. As to the conversation Wallace had with Beattie concerning the time of the call, the judge said 'it would, one imagines, be very dangerous to draw any inference seriously adverse, to the prisoner from that conversation'.

On the question of the mackintosh also Mr Justice Wright clearly leant in favour of the defendant:

One [theory] was that she was seated in that armchair, you remember, by the fireplace, and was struck down with a blow, and then, when she fell to the ground, the remaining blows were administered. That would mean that the assailant came to her and attacked her in front. Of course on that view I do not know that I ought to say it is not possible, but it is very difficult to think that the assailant was her husband, wearing a mackintosh. It is possible of course, but if he was not going out there and then, one asks why did he put on the mackintosh, why did she light the fire; and if she lighted the fire under the impression that he was not going out and they were going to have some music, why should he be wearing his mackintosh?

On the question of the blood the judge said:

Whoever did the crime, the evidence seems conclusive, must have been very seriously splashed with blood. There was a very bad wound and one of the arteries had been severed, and it is quite obvious from that picture, and also from the photos, that there must have been a great deal of blood splashed about. How in the world was it possible that the murderer, whoever he was, left no trace behind?

On the subject of the time factor Mr Justice Wright referred to the evidence of Close and also that of Wildman and Jones. The medical evidence he dismissed as being of little assistance. He saw little significance in the missing iron bar and poker and said that Wallace's search for the bogus address did not necessarily point to him having committed the crime. Nor did he attach much importance to the problem over the locks.

At the conclusion of his summing up there could be no doubt at all that Mr Justice Wright had summed up for an acquittal, The shock was therefore all the greater when, after only one hour's retirement the jury returned with a verdict of 'guilty'.

Wallace's reaction was to say, 'I am not guilty, I do not want to say any more'.

CHAPTER NINE

THE MEANING OF CIRCUMSTANTIAL EVIDENCE

There are two kinds of evidence: direct and circumstantial. Suspicion, however strong, must be rejected by the jury. It is a common myth that what is referred to as 'mere circumstantial' evidence is an inferior form of testimony. Nothing could be further from the truth. In fact in the majority of murder trials there is no direct evidence which the prosecution can advance against the accused; no one to say that they saw the actual killers; no written confession by the defendant; still less likely a confession in open court, as sometimes happens in television dramas. The unique element in the Wallace case is that the evidence is not merely circumstantial. It lends itself to two distinct interpretations – one prejudicial to the defendant and the other favourable. In this short chapter, therefore, I propose to introduce the reader to a brief study of the subject: by quoting the words of Mr Justice Wright in his summing up; looking at what the English courts have said about it in recent years; and discussing some of the famous criminal trials where circumstantial evidence has been a vital factor in the question of guilt or innocence.

At the end of the Wallace trial Mr Justice Wright said this:

> It is a most remarkable murder, but there it is. There is no doubt that the woman was murdered, and there is no doubt that whoever did it covered up his traces, and evaded leaving behind any sort of trace whatever. There it is. There is certainly no eye-witness, except the actual murderer, besides the dead woman, and therefore the evidence in this case, and the evidence that can be brought against anybody here, is purely circumstantial. You know, in many cases, especially of murder, the only evidence that is available is circumstantial evidence, but circumstantial evidence may vary in value almost infinitely. There is some circumstantial evidence which is as good and conclusive as the evidence of the actual eye-witness. In other cases the only circumstantial evidence which anyone can present still leaves loopholes and doubts, and still leaves possibilities of other explanations, of other persons and still leaves the charge against the accused man little more than a probability and nothing that could be described as reasonably conclusive. If I might give you an illustration, supposing you have a room with one door and a closed window and a passage leading from that door, and a man comes up the passage, goes through the door into the room and finds another man standing with a pistol, and on the floor a dead man; the circumstantial evidence there would be almost conclusive, if not conclusive.

If on the other hand, the conditions being much the same, there was an intruder who, hearing the pistol shot went into the room, and if there was another door and he went in and found a man holding the pistol, it might be perfectly consistent with his having gone in, and the actual murderer being outside the door. The real test of circumstantial evidence is: does it exclude every reasonable possibility? I can even put it higher: Does it exclude other theories or possibilities? If you cannot put the evidence against the accused man beyond a probability and nothing more, if that is a probability which is not inconsistent with there being other reasonable probabilities, then it is impossible for a jury to say: We are satisfied beyond reasonable doubt that the charge is made out against the accused man . A man cannot be convicted of any crime, least of all murder, merely on probabilities, unless they are so strong as to amount to a reasonable certainty. If you have other possibilities, a jury would not, and I believe ought not, to come to the conclusion that the charge is established.

Then again the question is not: who did this crime? the question is: did the prisoner do it? – or rather to put it more accurately: is it proved to your reasonable satisfaction and beyond all reasonable doubt that the prisoner did it? It is a fallacy to say: If the prisoner did not do it, who did? It is a fallacy to look at it and say it is very difficult to think the prisoner did not do it. Who did? And it may be equally difficult to think the prisoner did do it. The prosecution must discharge the onus cast upon them of establishing the guilt of the prisoner, and must go far beyond suspicion or surmise, or even probability, unless the probability is such as to amount to a practical certainty; and when a jury is considering circumstantial evidence, they must always bear these considerations in mind, and must not be led by any extraneous considerations to act upon what cannot be regarded as – well I cannot say mere suspicion – but cannot be regarded as establishing beyond all reasonable doubt the guilt of the accused man .

Now let us see what the English courts have said on the subject.

In the case of *Ellwood* in 1908 the Appeal Court said that facts that tend to prove or negative a person's capacity to do an act into which the court is enquiring may be highly relevant. The accused's knowledge of the effect of certain drugs, his skill in their applications and his ability to procure them would be admissible evidence at his trial for murder by means of their use. The absence of these factors would be admissible on his behalf.

This subject has been pronounced upon in a number of cases since the Wallace trial. In *Teper,* in 1952, Lord Normand said:

Circumstantial evidence is receivable in criminal as well as civil cases, and indeed the necessity of admitting such evidence is more obvious in the former than in the latter, for, in criminal cases, the possibility of proving the matter charged by the direct and positive testimony of eye-witnesses or by conclusive documents is much more rare than in civil cases, and where such evidence is not available the jury are permitted to infer from the facts proved other facts necessary to complete the elements of guilt or establish innocence.

It must always be narrowly examined, if only because evidence of this kind may be fabricated to cast suspicion on another.... It is also necessary before drawing the inference of the accused's guilt from circumstantial evidence to be sure that there are no other co-existing circumstances which would weaken or destroy the inference.

In the case of *Plamp* in 1963 Mr Justice Channell said:

... facts that supply a motive for a particular act – such as that a man who was engaged to another woman on the basis that he was already a widower and then murdered his wife may even be used to prove the commission of the act so motivated. This is among the items of circumstantial evidence most often admitted. So far as lack of motive is concerned there was a great deal of difference between absence of proved motive and proved absence of motive.

In the case of *Broahurst* which was before the Court of Appeal in 1964 Lord Denning said:

A fact may be relevant to a fact in issue because it throws light on it by reason or proximity in time or circumstance. This is frequently expressed by the statement that the relevant fact is part of the *res gestae* [the association of things]. The doctrine is mainly concerned with the admissibility of statements made contemporaneously with the occurrence of some act or event into which the court is enquiring. As a matter of everyday reasoning the evidence against a man may be greatly strengthened by his failure to give a prompt explanation of conduct proved or alleged against him, or by the inadequacy of his explanation. If on the proved facts, two inferences may be drawn about the accused's conduct or state of mind, his untruthfulness is a factor which the jury can properly take into account in strengthening the inference of guilt.

In the House of Lords case of *McGreevy* in 1993 it was said:

Where circumstantial evidence is the basis for the prosecution case, the direction to the jury needs to be in special form, provided always that in suitable terms it is made plain to them that they must not convict unless they are satisfied beyond all reasonable doubt; a jury can readily understand that from one piece of evidence which they accept various inferences might be drawn, and it requires no more than ordinary common sense for a jury to understand that if one suggested inference leads to a conclusion of guilt and another suggested inference leads to a suggestion of innocence, they could not on that piece of evidence alone be satisfied of guilt beyond all reasonable doubt unless they wholly rejected and excluded the latter suggestion; furthermore a jury can fully understand that if a fact which they accept is inconsistent with guilt or may be so they could not say they were satisfied of guilt beyond all reasonable doubt.

These then are the principles laid down by the courts. Let us see how they were applied in some of the famous trials of the last century, and compare those cases and the verdicts reached with that of Wallace.

Arthur Devereux was a chemist's assistant who in 1905 was charged with the murder of his wife and their two twin children. He had married his wife in 1898 and prior to the birth of the twins a son had been born. The burden of supporting a large family on a small income drove Devereux to despair. He brought home a tin trunk and poisoned his wife and the twins by means of a bottle of morphine, He then placed the bodies in a trunk which was taken to a warehouse in Harrow. Arthur then left the area where he lived and moved to another part of London. Unfortunately for him, his mother-in-law became suspicious and called in the police. When the investigations began Arthur moved to Coventry. He was traced there through a piano hire company to whom he had failed to keep up his payments. When interviewed by police he replied 'You are making a mistake, I don't know anything about a tin trunk'. Up to that point the police had not made any mention of the trunk.

The defence Devereux put forward was that his wife had killed the twins and then committed suicide. He claimed that he had disposed of the bodies because he did not consider the police would treat him fairly during their investigation.

The points on which his conviction rested were, firstly his statement on arrest, and secondly his description of himself in a job application as a widower given while his wife was still alive. He was executed, protesting his innocence to the last.

The case of Oscar Slater in 1908 was a classic instance of a police force being under pressure to find the culprit, yet having little or no evidence to rely upon. Marion Gilchrist, an elderly lady living alone in her flat in Glasgow was murdered in a similar manner to Julia Wallace. She was beaten about her head, and from her apartment a brooch was stolen. Slater was a German Jew who was a gambling den operator and had a record of pimping prostitutes. The only evidence against him was identification by a very unreliable witness, and the fact that he had pawned a brooch – for which there was no evidence that it was the stolen piece of jewellery. Slater was convicted and sentenced to death. His sentence was reduced to life imprisonment but it was only after many years that he was ultimately reprieved and awarded compensation.

The case of Dr Hawsley Harvey Crippen in 1910 was a classic example of circumstantial evidence bringing a man to the gallows. Crippen's marriage to his wife Cora had deteriorated. They quarrelled over money, and Cora, who was an aspiring but unsuccessful actress, was sexually promiscuous. Crippin himself began a relationship with Ethel le Neve, a younger woman than himself. There was no direct evidence about how Crippen murdered his wife, but Cora disappeared, and Crippen gave different accounts as to what had happened to her. He claimed that she had gone to the mountains of California; that she had left him for another man and that she had been taken to hospital with double pneumonia.

Crippen, who had travelled with Ethel on a trip to Dieppe, sent a telegram to a friend saying that Cora had died. Suspicion led to investigation and the remains of Cora were discovered in the cellar at Hilldrop Crescent in London where Crippen lived. A warrant was issued for Crippen's arrest, but he and Ethel had sailed for America. They were arrested on arrival. Crippen was convicted and hanged, Ethel le Neve was acquitted.

If ever a man was trapped by circumstantial evidence it was Crippen. His defence that the human remains in the cellar were there when he moved into the house in Hilldrop Crescent was destroyed by the forensic analysis of Bernard Spilsburg which identified the remnants of pyjamas as having been made after Crippen moved in. The various explanations given for her disappearance, the telegram announcing her death and above all Crippen's flight to America with Ethel sealed his fate. Crippen went to the gallows protesting his innocence, as have other convicted murderers.

Frederick Henry Seddon was convicted of the murder of Miss Eliza Barrow in 1912 on circumstantial evidence which, in retrospect, appears anything but strong. Seddon, like Wallace, was an insurance agent and was preoccupied with money. He bought the house at 63 Tollington Park which had three floors, and let the top floor to Eliza Barrow, an elderly wealthy spinster. Miss Barrow's health began to deteriorate and she took to her bed. Fly papers impregnated with arsenic were placed in her room to control the flies. She became worse and died. Seddon arranged a very hasty funeral for her. Eliza had transferred money to Seddon for the purchase of annuities and had changed her will making him sole executor. Miss Barrow's family, who knew nothing of her death, became suspicious and informed the police. Seddon was arrested, and made a truly terrible impression on the jury when he gave evidence. He was convicted and executed. His wife, although clearly involved, was acquitted

A most unusual form of circumstantial evidence was presented to a jury in the case of George Smith in June 1915. This concerned what was known as the 'brides in the bath' murders. Smith, who was one of the early serial killers of the 20th century, had a record of fraud and dishonesty. He discovered a way of making money by murder. He married a succession of women, and, having obtained their money by trickery or taking out life policies on their lives, then proceeded to drown them in their baths. Spilsbury, then at the height of his fame, had demonstrated at a re-enactment prior to the trial, how a person could be drowned by pulling the feet suddenly so that their head becomes suddenly immersed. When first tried this nearly had fatal results with a volunteer. It greatly impressed the jury who sent an unrepentant Smith to his execution.

more info re Spils-bury?

There have been few more controversial cases than that of Frederick Bywaters and Edith Thompson in December 1922. Percy and Edith Thompson, a married couple, befriended Freddy Bywaters, a young merchant seaman. They went on holiday together, and, as may happen in a dangerous three-cornered arrangement, a passionate relationship developed between Edith and Bywaters. When Bywaters was away at sea Edith wrote to him a number of letters which mentioned the question of how Percy could be got rid of. There may have been a strong element of fantasy on Edith's side, but Bywaters took the letters sufficiently seriously to attack and stab Percy to death when Edith and Percy were together in the street. Notwithstanding evidence that at the time of the attack she was heard to shout, 'Oh don't', and when confronted by Bywaters at the police station said 'Oh god, oh god! What can I do? Why did he do it? I didn't want him to do it. I must tell the truth', Edith was convicted as an accessory to murder and dragged in a drugged state to the scaffold. This case was instrumental in the subsequent cessation of capital punishment. Edith's letters to Bywaters were the basis of the circumstantial evidence with led to her execution.

CHAPTER TEN

THE APPEAL

The verdict of guilty came as a surprise to many, and a shock to those who supported Wallace. The summing up by the judge was unmistakably in favour of an acquittal. Yet juries can be notoriously unpredictable. They do not always follow the judge when, in so far as he is able within the parameters of his duty, he expresses his view of the evidence. Sometimes a judge who expresses himself or herself too forcefully in favour of one side or the other obtains the opposite result to that which is hoped for. Juries are invariably directed by the judge that they must reach their decision on the evidence alone, and avoid any feelings of prejudice which they may have formed. But this can be a counsel of perfection. Every effort is made during a trial to prevent the members of the jury having contact with the outside world, but there is no way of knowing whether their minds have been influenced before the case by conversation with other people who have already acquired fixed views, which many people are inclined to do. Moreover they may have read newspaper and other reports of police investigations and preliminary proceedings.

Any comments made by a judge on the evidence are invariably followed by such words as, 'I will direct you regarding the law, but the facts are entirely for you'. Yet it is a myth that juries attend only to the hard facts revealed by the evidence. They are heavily influenced by the demeanour of the defendant if he or she gives evidence on their own behalf, and if they fail to do so the jury will wonder why. In the cases of Seddon, Armstrong and Edith Thompson, where the case for the prosecution was not strong, it is certainly arguable that had they not gone into the witness box they may well not have been convicted. In his very fully researched book *The Killing of Julia Wallace*, Jonathan Goodman writes on the subject of possible prejudice on the part of the jury:

> Roland Oliver's belief, expressed to Schofield Allen and Munroe on the second night of the trial, that the jury were not listening to the evidence, had been proved true. By finding Wallace guilty they had brought in a verdict against themselves. It was clear now that most of the members of the jury, if not all of them, had decided the case before they ever entered the box.
>
> Soon after the committal proceedings, knowing that local opinion was strong against Wallace, Hector Munroe had considered applying for a writ of Certiorari to have the case tried in another part of the country; but after being as-

sured by the prosecuting solicitor's office that no one from Liverpool would be chosen to serve on the jury, he had not done so. This was a mistake.

The jury was mainly composed of people from Southport, Warrington, Widnes and St Helens – all four towns within fifteen miles of Liverpool, well within earshot of the rumours connecting Wallace with the murder; all four towns within the circulation areas of the Liverpool evening papers, which published verbatim reports of the one sided evidence given at the magistrate's court. This was bad enough, but to make it worse, at least two of the jurors were resident in Liverpool at the time, although their addresses on the jury list showed them to be living elsewhere.

The date for Wallace's execution was fixed for the 12th May, but this was respited when the appeal date was set at the 18th. The prospects were not good. Wallace had only two hopes of success: The Criminal Appeal Act of 1907 and the Home Secretary's power of reprieve. The latter, in the light of the nature and violence of the crime was highly unlikely. With regard to the former there was only a slim chance. Since the passing of the Act only on two occasions had the Court of Appeal allowed appeals against convictions. The 1907 Act contained the words: 'Provided that the court of criminal appeal may dismiss the appeal if they think that no substantial miscarriage of justice has occurred'.

The corollary to this applied when a substantial miscarriage of justice had occurred. How could this be shown to have happened? The grounds of appeal were very limited. These were usually misdirection of the jury by the judge in his summing up or the submission of fresh evidence which was not produced at the trial. The court was very loath to interfere with the verdict of a jury. Furthermore the other alternatives available, namely reduction of the charge to manslaughter or the substitution of life imprisonment in place of the death penalty, were most improbable, having regard to the ferocity of the murder.

While Wallace languished in the condemned cell, Schofield, Allen and Munroe prepared the grounds of appeal:

1. The verdict was unreasonable and cannot be supported having regard to the evidence. The whole of the evidence was consistent with Wallace's innocence and the prosecution never discharged the burden of proving that he and no one else was guilty.

2. The judge at the conclusion of the evidence should have withdrawn the case from the jury.

3. Misstatements were made by the prosecution in the opening speech.

4. No motive was suggested by the prosecution.

5. A great feature was made that Wallace's demeanour on 20 January 1931, was cool, calm and indifferent. No such suggestion was made at the police court, though all the same witnesses were examined.

6. An effort was made to suggest that the mackintosh was worn by the assailant.

7. Professor MacFall forced upon the court the suggestion that this was a crime of frenzy, thus supplying the jury with a reason for the commission by Wallace of this murder.

8. Wallace was prejudiced by the fact that the crown failed to call as witnesses for the prosecution Wildman and Jones, and also failed to supply the defence with copies of all statements taken from persons who were not called at the police court.

9. The judge in his summing up, misdirected the jury by saying that if there was no motive for Wallace, there was no motive for anyone else.

10. On the occasion of the speeches by the prosecuting solicitor at the Liverpool City Police Court, the said prosecuting solicitor made a number of misstatements as to the evidence and the case for the prosecution… Which said statements were reported in extense and widely circulated throughout Liverpool and the surrounding districts, and which, although in the end disposed of, were nevertheless prejudicial.

Hemmerde and Oliver reiterated the arguments which they had employed before the Liverpool jury, but without offering any theories. Hemmerde insisted that the cumulative circumstantial evidence pointed to Wallace as the killer. Oliver maintained that the case for the Crown was nothing more than a collection of suppositions. The court was presided over by Lord Hewart, the Lord Chief Justice, who was known for the confidence he placed in the jury system. The other two judges were Mr Justice Hawke and Mr Justice Branson.

At the conclusion of counsel's submissions the three judges retired to consider their decision. This was unusual since the Court of Criminal Appeal generally came to its conclusion without retirement. The onlookers, including a deathly pale Wallace, awaited the result. The Lord Chief Justice delivered the judgment of the court:

The appellant William Herbert Wallace was charged at the Assizes in Liverpool with the murder of his wife on January 20th. In the result he was convicted, and on April 25th last he was sentenced to death. He now appeals against that conviction. Three facts are obvious. The first is that at the conclusion of the case for the crown no submission was made on behalf of the appellant that there was no case to go to the jury. The second fact which seems to be obvious is, that the evidence was summed up by the learned judge with complete fairness and accuracy, and it would not have been at all surprising if the result had been an acquittal of the prisoner. The third obvious fact is that the case is one eminently of difficulty and doubt.

Now the whole of the material evidence has been closely and critically examined before us, and it does not appear to me to be necessary to discuss it again. Suffice it to say, that we are not concerned here with suspicion, however grave, or with theories, however ingenious. Section 4 of the Criminal Appeal Act of 1907 provides that the Court of Criminal Appeal shall allow the appeal if they think that the verdict of the jury should be set aside on the ground that it cannot be supported having regard to the evidence. The conclusion at which we have arrived is, that the case against the appellant, which we have carefully and anxiously considered and discussed, was not proved with that certainty which is necessary in order to justify a verdict of guilty, and therefore it is our duty to take the course indicated by the section of the statute to which I have referred. The result is that this appeal will be allowed and the conviction quashed.

CHAPTER ELEVEN

WALLACE: A FREE MAN

Wallace had been cleared – or had he? The quashing of a conviction by the Court of Criminal Appeal was not the same thing as an acquittal by a jury. In fact it was similar in its effect to a comparable ruling today by the Court of Appeal that a finding by a jury be set aside on the ground that it is 'unsafe'. The appeal court was not saying that Wallace was innocent. It said that the evidence produced by the prosecution did not merit a conviction – a very different thing. Wallace had been given his life back, but the aftermath of suspicion and innuendo was unavoidable. He tried to pick up the shattered pieces of his previous life. He continued to live at 29 Wolverton Street, a somewhat strange decision in the light of the horrific events which happened there. He resumed his work for the Prudential, but although some of his old colleagues were kindly and sympathetic, others were less generous in their attitudes, and people with whom he had been on friendly terms started to avoid him. Eventually the situation became intolerable and Wallace retired to a bungalow in the Cheshire countryside.

If there is any validity in the suggestion that Wallace's conduct was strange at the time of the murder, the same could be said for his behaviour afterwards. He took to writing about his life and experiences, which surely must be almost unprecedented for a man who had been fortunate to escape the gallows. One would have thought that in such a situation most people would seek anonymity and forgetfulness. Wallace turned author. His writings are contained in three sources. The first is his 'life story', the second a series of five articles written for the *John Bull Magazine* in 1932, and the third is his private diary.

There can be little doubt that he was paid for his contribution to John Bull. At the time of Julia's murder he possessed £152. Two years later, when he died, the figure was £1,196 – a sum equivalent to nearer £10,000 in today's money. In this chapter it is proposed to examine these writings and then to contemplate what appears to have been the psychological state which prompted Wallace to produce them. Let it be said emphatically that nothing from the pen of Wallace contributes in the slightest to the case against him, nor is there a word amounting to anything approaching a confession. Quite the contrary. But to obtain a clear picture of the man and his thoughts and motivation they cannot be left out. This is important because there appears to be no other case of an acquitted, reprieved or released on appeal, alleged murderer who has subsequently written about his experiences as fully as Wallace.

Let us begin with some passages from his 'Life Story', quoted by Wyndham-Brown in *The Trial of William Herbert Wallace*:

I was born in the year 1878. We lived in the Lakeland district and my early days were spent in that glorious country of mountain, lake and fell. What dreamed I, a happy innocent child – of all the horrors which were to meet me forty years further down the road of Life?

At fourteen years of age I was apprenticed, for five years to the drapery trade. After several assistantships in various towns, the wanderlust which had obsessed me in earlier years grew to fever heat, and at the age of twenty three I sailed for India, to take a position as a salesman in Calcutta.

Sentenced to death for a third time by a council of doctors, I had to leave India, and seek the milder climates of China. In Shanghai I worked as an advertising Manager for a general store. My illness however, reached its climax, and I made up my mind to leave China and return at once to England. If I had to die I preferred the land of my birth as my final resting place. I arrived home seriously ill, and entered Guy's Hospital. My weakness prevented me from doing any work at all for eighteen months, but my financial position becoming somewhat precarious, I took a situation in Manchester. During this time I had begun to take an interest in politics, addressing meetings in all parts of the North Lonsdale Constituency. To my delight I was eventually appointed Liberal Agent for the Rippon Division, West Riding, of Yorkshire. Here began the happiest years of my life, for in Harrogate I met at this time my future wife. She was a lady of good birth and social position, whose tastes were very similar to my own, Dark haired, dark eyed, full of energy and vivaciousness, she filled in every corner of the picture I had dreamed of that one woman in all the world most men enshrine in their hearts . She was an excellent pianist, no mean artist in water-colour, a fluent French scholar, and of cultured literary taste. The courtship lasted two years and was idyllic. From the first moment we met we found in each other friendship, companionship and love we needed.

Those were days when all the world and the future seemed rose coloured, sun-like and steeped in everlasting happiness. Nothing could ever change! But through this Eldorado of a lover's dream the wheel of fate was turning, turning...

A blissful year of marriage preceded the outbreak of the Great War. We set up house in a quiet neighbourhood of Harrogate, little dreaming of the maelstrom that was destined to uproot us within a few months. The war crashing into our quiet lives brought politics to the ground, and I was once again thrown on my beam ends. I was fortunate in securing employment as a district agent with the Prudential Assurance Company, and my wife and I moved to Liverpool, taking up our residence at 29 Wolverton Street.

Here we lived in perfect happiness and harmony for sixteen years. Our days and months and years were filled with complete enjoyment, placid perhaps, but with all the happiness of quietude and mutual interest and affection. Neither of us cared very much for entertaining other people or for being entertained; we were sufficient in ourselves. My wife had an artistic natural love of colour, landscape, seascape, and flowers to appeal to her and I looked at all things with the eyes of a naturalist.

As a young man I had played chess. In Liverpool I continued this pastime, and the only times alone in our little home was to visit the chess club at the City Café, to deliver my lectures at the technical college, or to attend to my insurance business. On all other occasions my wife was my inseparable companion.

All those happy industrious years the wheel of fate was turning towards the crowning tragedy of my ill-starred life…

There is little or nothing in the passages to throw much light on the inner character of Wallace. Perhaps the most significant words are 'the crowning tragedy of my ill-starred life'. He already sees his life as 'ill-starred' before the time of his wife's murder. This, notwithstanding the 'idyllic' happiness he enjoyed with his wife for 16 years. Some of the people who had contact with the Wallace's confirmed that their marriage was placid and content to all appearances. Others who knew them took a different view. Wallace's extreme frugality over money was undoubtedly one of his characteristics. He acquired expensive things for himself such as his violin and his microscope, but people who were familiar with Julia said she looked dowdy and always wore the same clothes over the years. Further, let it be known that after her death money was found sewn into her underclothes. Even making allowances for his poor health, Wallace was a man of very little education who wandered from job to job before his employment with the Prudential. Yet he describes himself as a 'naturalist'. He writes of his lectures at the Technical College in Liverpool. Yet he had no qualifications of a technical or scientific kind whatever. Did he lecture on the basis of some amateur home-based experiments?

In his reference to the 'wheel of fate' turning he depicts himself as a helpless pawn in the hands of a cruel destiny. His description of his wife's charms and talents make it clear that he felt he had married 'well', but we have little or no information as to whether he benefited financially from the wedlock.

With regard to the diaries, the extracts we shall consider are both before and after Julia's death:

13 February 1929:

On the way home with – had a discussion on religion. I find he is, like myself, indifferent to the dogmas and rituals of the churches and chapels, and agree that if there is a hereafter the man without any so called religious beliefs, and a non- church attender, but who lives a decent life, and who abstains from telling lies, or cheating, or acts of meanness, and who honestly tries to do good, has as much chance of getting there as the professed Christian who attends his place of worship regularly.

20 March 1929:

Listened to 'The Master Builder' by Ibsen. This is a fine thing, and shows clearly how a man may build up a fine career, and as the world has it, be a great success, and yet in his own mind feels that he has been an utter failure, and how ghastly a mistake he has made to sacrifice love, and the deeper comforts of life in order to achieve success. Curious that Julia did not seem to appreciate this play! I feel sure she did not grasp the inner significance and real meaning of the play.

9 September 1929:

At four o'clock Julia and I left for home, but getting lost we had to return to Settle, so that it was five o'clock before we really got away. The roads were crowded with cars, and at Clitheroe all cars were being held up for inspection of licences. Probably the police were trying to comb out in order to get some line on the motorist who ran down a police constable on the previous Thursday leaving him to die in the road. If they get him, I hope he gets ten years hard labour for his callousness.

26 October 1930:

No one has had any knowledge of a previous existence. If I previously existed as a thinking organism I probably argued much as I do now, and now that I am here, I recognise clearly that immortality means absolutely nothing to me. Any individuality I possessed formerly has gone. So, too, when I pass out of this existence, individual mortality is meaningless, unless I am able to retain something of my present, and that fact that my previous existence is now meaningless argues that the next existence also has no meaning for me. So why worry about a life hereafter which has no meaning for me.

6 November 1930:

The tournaments (chess) are now up, and I see I am in class three. This about represents my strength of play. I suppose I could play better, but I feel it is too much like hard work to go in for chess whole heartedly, hence my lack of practice keeps me in a state of mediocrity. Good enough for a nice game, but no good really for first class play.

The following extracts refer to the period during which Wallace was in custody and the later time during his residence at the bungalow in Cheshire.

At long last the date of the opening of the Assizes arrived. It is difficult for me to describe the feelings of an innocent man about to be put on trial for his life. There can be no position in human experience so terrible. Not to be able to convince one's fellows of the truth is a desperate situation – what does it count that one has been a truthful man all ones life? No torture of the inquisition could have rivalled this appalling sensation of being caught like a rat in a trap.

The actual day arrived and I was taken to the court for the trial. I hadn't the slightest idea how an Assize trial was conducted and in spite of the ordeal before me I was interested to see what it was like. Two warders stood with me at the foot of some steps leading to the dock, and from this position I could hear the jury being sworn in. I could see nothing except the ceiling of the courts, but part of the oath as administered to each juryman came to my ears and fixed itself in my memory 'and true deliverance make before our sovereign Lord the King' the words true deliverance rang in my ears with a soothing sound. That was what I wanted. The truth – a true deliverance out of that hell ... and then came the words of the clerk of the court ... Put up Wallace.

I was asked if I pleaded guilty or not guilty, 'Not Guilty' I said.

I meant to make my reply as emphatic as possible. If it were only possible to make the truth sound true; People talk glibly about words ringing true. But do they? I had determined that nothing should cause me to show emotion; that the vile and unjust charge should be met with all the dignity I could command.

Wallace then goes on to describe his feelings on being convicted of murder and sentenced to death:

The jury retired, and I was taken down the steps to the corridor below the court. Then began a distressing period of nerve strain. As the minutes dragged by, and I was not called up, I began to wonder what the jury were discussing. The fact that they were remaining out of court for a prolonged period was surely against my interests and boded ill for me. My anticipations proved to be all too correct. Forty minutes crept slowly on leaden feet and then the summons came. Once more I stood within that railed dock.

How can I describe my feelings then? One idea was dominant in my mind – to retain my dignity whatever the verdict might be. I could feel emotions no more. Never again should I be able to trust my fellow men. This was a world of evil into which by some strange chance I had wandered. I was a stranger – I did not belong.

The court was tense and deadly silent as the Clerk of Assize turned to the jury, and asked them if they were agreed upon their verdict. A terrible pause – a blank – nothingness – in which all the world stood still.

Guilty

If I had any feelings, they were those which one might imagine a fly might have, caught in a web and unable to break loose. To this moment I do not know what I said. I was looking into a blank space. The judge made not the slightest comment, but in a slow and rather low voice pronounced sentence of death. The chaplain's Amen came to me in the faintest whisper. I had been sentenced to death.

I was hustled down the steps and into a cell below where my dinner was bought to me, I could not even look at it. My whole being was sick with despair. The shadow of the gallows was black and very close. In about an hour's time I was rushed back to Walton Jail, and this time was taken direct to the cell reserved for prisoners condemned to death. I was surrounded by officials and compelled to change into the grey convict uniform prescribed by law. This bought home to me with savage grimness, the hopelessness of my position.

For the first time I broke down completely and wept. I found I was to be under the constant eyes of two officers day and night, who would live with me in the cell ... until a certain morning at eight o'clock. During the long night I tossed and turned in my bed but could not sleep. There were the grim sentinels of death sitting in easy chairs reading. The light came from outside the cell through thick glass let into slots in the walls. I could not sleep

From Saturday when I was sentenced to death until midday on Monday I lived in a state of extreme nervous tension. The most appalling shock of all came when the governor visited me and announced that the date for my execution had been fixed. From that moment I was dazed. It struck me that although one has heard so much of the laws delays in my case the law had lost no time. It seemed as if it was eager and panting for my blood.

One doubts whether a more graphic account has ever been given by a condemned man of his feelings after conviction and sentence. Guilty or innocent Wallace attracts a degree of sympathy at his miserable plight. Yet here again the mystery continues. Could a man be guilty of such a crime and yet write with such colour and in such moving tones about his ordeal. Either he is a terribly wronged man, placed in an intolerable situation by a flawed system of justice, or he is a vicious criminal with an amazing gift for self-exoneration. There is no third alternative.

Or is there? Is there just the possibility that a man may commit a terrible deed and then, in the full flood of remorse and shock afterwards, experience a mysterious mechanism of the mind which blocks it out and produces amnesia to the extent that the person concerned comes to believe that the event has not occurred. This is an interesting psychological aspect which we should consider a little later on.

Wallace speaks of his feelings during the period between conviction and appeal:

After dinner, half an hour's walking in some quiet portion of the grounds. On this walk there was a long narrow garden built up against the wall and here were planted lupins, irises, delphiniums and other flowers. The irises during my last walk there were just about to burst into flower and I used to wonder if I should see them in full bloom, and if they would be the last flowers I should see on this earth.

A fortnight elapsed and then I received a notification that the date of hearing of my appeal had been fixed for May 18th, and that I was to be taken to Pentonville Jail.

Wallace takes up the story of the appeal in his diary;

16 May 1931:

Left Walton for Pentonville guarded by officers. Had to submit to handcuffs which were not taken off until I was safely in Pentonville. A taxi took me up the Lime Street platform, I had only a few yards to cross to the reserved carriage with drawn blinds. Even so it had obviously leaked out, as there were a number of railway officials and some of the public present. Strange how this morbid curiosity draws people, who, if they only reflect must know it is a torture to the person under observation. Going down in the train I was greatly impressed by the green and wonderful beauty of the country. I had seen little but high walls and iron barred windows for about sixteen weeks, and it was something to cheer me, and take my mind off the grim horrors of my position. The officers did their best to make me comfortable.

Entering Pentonville was a melancholy ordeal The prison is grim and forbidding and I felt despondent and depressed beyond measure. Here again was that never ending jingling of keys – symbols of despair had they become. I was searched, and then re-clothed and marched off to the condemned cell. I was a prey to the deepest dejection. I had little hope that my appeal would succeed. I knew if my appeal was dismissed my chance of a reprieve was slight.

18 May 1931:

Day of my appeal, Off to court at 10.30. Handcuffed but in my own clothes. At 11am I was called to appear, and once again I faced the court. This time my position was undeniably grave. After five hours the court adjourned and I was taken back to Pentonville.

19 May 1931:

After the close of counsels' speeches the Lord Chief Justice said their Lordships would retire for a short while to consider their decision. I was taken out of court into the corridor behind and there for about an hour I paced two and fro, alternately hopeful and depressed. It was a terrible strain. Freedom or death awaited me, and I had become insensible to all other considerations. Minute after minute passed by and I now began to think that the long wait was in my favour, in contrast to the long wait at the Assizes when I felt the delay was against me.

At last their lordships returned and I was again taken into the dock. The court was hushed to an almost uncanny silence. No one moved nor a paper rustled. The very breathing of all there seemed suspended. After what seemed an eternity of time the Lord Chief Justice began to deliver judgement. I could not follow all he said, my mind lost all receptiveness and all I remember is that my obsession to betray no emotion was as strong as ever. Tensely I waited, oblivious to all but that slow, dreadfully slow utterance of the Lord Chief Justice. I could not grasp all he said, my brain refused to function. It was as if I was suspended in space and detached from everything. Slowly, slowly went on the voice, miles away as it were, and then I heard the Lord Chief Justice end by saying: The Court allows the appeal and the conviction of the court below is quashed?

Was it true or were my ears mocking me? Immediately there began a buzz, and the beginning of a cheer, instantly suppressed. Then I realised I had won, and that I was free.

It is impossible not to be impressed by Wallace's striking description of the worst hours of his life. The remaining entries in the diaries refer in the main to his new home and garden which he now inhabited in Cheshire, his loneliness without Julia and the suspicious and unforgiving attitude of others who have formed opinions of the case which are adverse to Wallace. However, in the entry for 14 September 1931 we find, for the first time, Wallace indicating that he knows the identity of the killer of his wife:

Just as I was going to dinner Parry stopped me, and said he wanted to talk to me for a few minutes. It was a desperately awkward position. Eventually I decided not to hear what he had to say. I told him I would talk to him some day, and give him something to think about. He must realise that I suspect him of the terrible crime. I fear I let him see clearly what I thought, and it may unfortunately put him on his guard. I wonder if it is any good putting a private detective on his track in the hope of something coming to light, I am more than half persuaded to try it.

6 October 1931:

I cannot disguise from myself that I am dreadfully nervous about entering the house after dark, I suppose it is because my nerves are all so shattered after the ordeal, and this, together with the recurring fits of grief and anguish over my dear Julia's end make me horribly depressed and apprehensive. Left to myself I am for ever trying to visualize what really did happen. Although I am convinced Parry killed her, yet it is difficult to get proof. It would be a great relief if he could only be caught, and the foul murder brought home to him .

The allegations against Richard Gordon Parry will be explored in the next chapter.

Why did Wallace publish articles about his life after his release? It has been said on his behalf that the articles were 'ghosted', but the fact remains that Wallace approved them and received payments.

Throughout his writings for the press Wallace, as would be expected, repeatedly asserts his innocence and continually reiterated the blissful quality of his marriage to Julia. Who did he think he was addressing and why?

Some of these articles are revealing of the state of mind of Wallace at this time. If he really believed that prejudice and suspicion were on every side, surely he must have realised that to draw attention to himself in this way could only make matters worse:

> I was free – free of God's good air like the rest of men, instead of languishing in a narrow cell waiting for a shameful death.
>
> Yet it was not the actual thought of death that had appalled me. It was the dread that an innocent man, should pass out and only remain in other men's minds as the author of an atrocious crime. I craved to have my good name given back to me.
>
> Restored now to my fellow creatures and the workaday world, I thought, in my simplicity, that they would share my joy, would hasten and never hesitate in the future, to congratulate me.

This seems to be too optimistic to be in the realm of reality.

> Alas! I know now by the bitter experience of the past twelve months that the world is more than willing to brand a man as guilty than acclaim him as innocent.
>
> The greatest judges in the world may set me free. But in the streets, among my friends and acquaintances, there are those who still regard me as a creature to be shunned. The revelation fell like a thunderbolt upon me.

Another passage in the articles show a remarkable animosity towards women:

> Can it be true I often wonder to myself during my lonely evenings, that the sympathy, charity and pity which we are taught are natural attributes of women are only a sham, a myth.
>
> My own happy domestic life with my dear wife for eighteen years – did that mislead me as to the true nature of the sex? And are other men similarly misled?
>
> These are questions that force themselves upon me as the result of a bitter lesson I have learned in the past twelve months – the lesson that women can become deadly enemies of a man, even though he has taken no part in their lives.

Compared with their ferocity, the words of the judge at Liverpool who sentenced me to death ring in my ears like compassion itself. Some of these women were once on the friendliest terms with my wife and myself, but that has not prevented them from spreading hate and slander against me. Indeed the more friendly they used to be, the worse and more wicked has been the manner in which they have sought to pile up evil opinion against me.

The reminder of the time I dwelt in my old home was a period during which my nerves were to be racked as they never had been since the night I discovered my wife lying lifeless in the sitting-room. A walk through the streets of the neighbourhood became an arctic adventure. Everywhere was ice and a devastating cold – cold faces belonging to cold hearts.

In some of the entries Wallace considerably exaggerates his intellectual status:

How my wife would have revelled in the boxes of tricks with which I have equipped the home! When she was with me her passion for novelty and discovery gave me countless hours of joy in explaining, as far as I could, the great riddles of the universe, and the why and wherefore of the scientific marvels that govern our everyday life.

For many years I have been an investigator and was for long a teacher of chemistry. As I passed from practical to theoretical science my wife tried hard to keep pace with me in the new problems of physics.

Always when I declared that my early theories of relativity and what are now called atomic physics were not properly accepted, she insisted that eventually I would find them being proved true.

Are these words those of a man of science of undiscovered genius, or are they the fantasy dreams of a self-educated minor insurance official, bereft of any practical basis whatever?

On another of his interests he writes:

I get out my chessboard and chessmen. Chess was one of the passions of my life. Liverpool is a great chess playing centre, and I was well known in the circle.

I have no one to play with me now. But on some evenings I get out my board, put the pieces on the square, and settle down to work out difficult problems.

A minute or two passes. Then I, who have in the past matched my brain against some of the greatest players in the world, realise that I am not concentrating on the board, though I sat staring at it.

Pitting his brains against some of the greatest players in the world seems to consist of having taken part in an all-comers exhibition by a famous player on a visit to Liverpool.

Some shadow seems to rise between me and my beloved game. I suddenly draw back. I know what it is. Chess is mixed up now with the terrible drama of my life. Even my proficiency in my hobby was used against me.

Chess that has been so long my delight and recreation became in an instant a menace to my life.

Can you wonder then, that when I sit alone in the evenings with the chess-board in front of me, the shadow of the dock, the shadow of the judge in the black cap – yes, even the shadow of the scaffold itself, rises before my eyes?

I push away the chessboard as I have already pushed away the microscope.

Wallace writes about his interest in philosophy:

When I reached home I sank into my chair more dispirited than I had been for a long time. After a while I went to my bookshelves and took down my volume of the Meditations of Marcus Aurelius – a book that in the past had been my comfort on many occasions when I was out of joint with this world.

To me it is the Golden Book among all books. I have been steeped from boyhood in its teachings. I craved for it in my condemned cell – more than for food. By an unfortunate series of circumstances, it was the only book I wanted that I was unable to obtain during the month that I lay under sentence of death.

I hungered night and day for the consolation I should find in its pages. When sleep would not come, although I was mentally tired out, I used to think how just one page of Marcus Aurelius would sooth my mind and bring me sleep.

He writes about his violin:

With the echoes of this passage still in my ears (whatsoever any man either doth or saith thou must be good, not for any man's sake, but for thy nature's sake). I suddenly remembered my fiddle. Perhaps with the help of its strings I should be able to banish the memories that haunted me.

I had tried a number of times to recapture my interest in my violin playing but always the sight of the violin case brought back to me the horror of one evening. It was the only other object I remember seeing when I stumbled into the sitting-room of my house in Anfield to find my wife battered to death. Tonight I wondered if the sympathetic voice of the violin might close the wounds which this anniversary date had reopened.

My attempts to play were useless; I stood by the piano, above which hangs my wife's photograph. I closed my eyes, and as I have so often done, tried to make myself believe she was again occupying the piano-seat, and that I could hear her accompaniment beginning. I chose a Beethoven Sonata. My first chord quivered, broke and was lost, violin and bow dropped limp in my hands. I found myself staring at the photograph over the piano. My anniversaries! Choking, scorching, soul-searing, dates... And they are mine alone among the whole of mankind .

Is this genuine sadness. Or is it remorse disguised as sorrow?

Wallace relives the moment of his conviction:

It was on April 25th 1931, that I stood in the dock at the Liverpool Assizes and saw the black cap upon the head of Mr Justice Wright. When I woke on the morning of April 25th this year, almost before my eyes were open, the whole scene in detail flashed before me.

I seemed to see myself standing erect in the dock. I was all ready to step out into the street the instant, as I expected, the verdict Not Guilty was given. How clearly on this April 25th did I recall it all –the grin on the face of the prison officer who led me to the dock as he noticed me, hat in hand. And his remark Optimistic eh? It was all so vivid that I really believe I nodded again just as twelve months before I had answered him with a nod. Again I saw myself looking for the exit from the dock into the well of the court, and thinking that I would get a taxi from the rank outside the building I felt once more the hush that descended on the court as the Clerk of Assize rose to ask the foreman of the jury for their verdict.

Finally, Wallace provides for posterity his own version of the crime:

Now let me say this. I know the murderer. In the porch of the front door of this lonely home of mine I have fitted an electric switch and lamp. They are not there for the convenience of friendly visitors, because I have none, but a few of my trusted friends. These things have been placed there to safe-guard my life.

Each night when I return home from business in Liverpool I am on the alert for attack.

The position of the switch is known only to myself, and before I open my door I touch it so that the house outside and inside, and every recess where an assailant may be lurking are lit up. The figure which one day I fully expect to see crouching and ready to strike will be that of the man who murdered my wife.

He killed Mrs Wallace with such savagery that he is capable of, and his rea-son for attempting to remove me before I complete the only mission I have left in life to place him in the dock where I stood and in the condemned cell I occupied.

This is an extraordinary allegation. The police had fully investigated all the other homes of possible suspects with which Wallace had supplied them and had cleared them all.

Moreover they announced, after Wallace's release, that they had closed the book and had no intention of continuing the investigation. Why should Wallace have considered himself to be in any danger?

I will reconstruct the crime from the knowledge I have since obtained. I do not for a moment suggest that because the Court of Criminal appeal quashed my conviction the police would regard their dignity as publicly hurt if they now arrested the murderer. Yet I feel bitter because since my acquittal, they refuse to give my lawyer or myself any information as to whether, and how far they have carried on any investigation.

The police had announced that they were not conducting any further investigation into the case.

I must have been well known to the man who took my wife's life.

In the days that followed Mrs Wallace's death, when I was searching, possibly as intensely as the police for a clue to the identity of the murderer, my private thoughts were often focused on the man. I did not then mentally convict him; I innocently believed that to establish a charge of murder against anyone, justice demanded the known presence of a motive.

How sorely I was to be disillusioned when my own life was at stake! With what mixed memories of my decision not to implicate this man did I listen to the prosecuting counsel confessing that he could not show any reason why I should commit murder, yet demanding all the same that I should hang. Even after my liberty was given back to me it was some time before I could connect my suspect with the crime. There were many circumstances by which I could deduce his guilt, but my idea of fair play still demanded that I should be able to show his motive for committing the crime.

Then at last I discovered why he went to my house and killed my wife. He must have known my haunts, and it was easy for him to be sure when I would be at my chess club to receive the telephone message by which he lured me away from the neighbourhood of my home. In the large café which accommodates the club there is posted a list of forthcoming matches, the players, the hour and the date.

The murder took place on a Tuesday night. Often I had in my house on Tuesdays as much as £100 of my employer's money, which I paid in weekly on Wednesdays. He must have got to know this, and also that the money was usually kept in the cash box and where the box always was.

When I left the house he would have been watching me leave to depart. It was my wife's rigid rule not to admit strangers into the house when she was alone, and to this day it has been a cause of speculation how the man made his way inside. He must have been ready with a pretext to be allowed to wait until I returned. He followed my wife into the sitting room, and as she bent down and lit the gas fire he struck her, possibly with a spanner. The implement of murder was never discovered.

Note that Wallace is alleging that murder took place before and not during the theft.

He now had to kill her. To strike her again as she lay on the floor and him standing over would mean the upward spurting of blood. Two strides took him into the lobby, where he had observed my mackintosh hanging and he held it as a shield between him and her body while he belaboured her to death.

136

It is interesting to note that here Wallace is abandoning the theory advanced on his behalf at the trial that Mrs Wallace had placed the mackintosh around her shoulders to give some protection against the cold when she opened the door to her assailant, and that together with her skirt, it caught fire as she fell and brushed against the gas fire. In fact he is giving support to the prosecution proposition that the mackintosh was used by the murderer to protect himself from the spurting blood and was burned by the flames from the skirt when it was thrown over the body.

> She must have been felled as soon as she lit the fire and before she could regulate the flow of gas. It would have been at full blaze, and as he bent at the fire place the flames set alight the mackintosh. Then he would see that the bottom edge of her skirt was burning and, throwing the mackintosh down he must have dragged her away from the fire and on to part of the coat, leaving her in the position I found her.

> So intimate was the knowledge he had gained of my affairs that I can picture his surprise when he broke open the cupboard and cash box and found only £4 on a Tuesday night. The reason there was only £4 in the house was that at the end of the previous week I had not made my usual heavy insurance collections because I was in bed, as the police satisfied themselves, with a fever. And most of the money I had taken on the other days of the week had been disbursed to health insurance claimants. Of these facts the murderer was not aware.

Wallace has reached remarkably detailed conclusions as to how the murder was committed. Indeed his theory is compelling. But is it his own constructed account of what is possible, or is it based on the recollection of his own actions?

Wallace concludes his narrative by protesting that, as a teacher of science and chemistry, he had at his command other means of disposing of his wife without causing her pain or attracting suspicion. Presumably he is referring here to poison. But poisons generally cause considerable pain and frequently attract suspicion.

Now let us turn to the character and personality of Wallace and what, if any, bearing it has on the question of whether or not he murdered his wife. Had something happened which caused this inhibited and almost alarmingly self controlled man to explode into a storm of anger – yet plan a crime with cold deliberation?

In his book *Beating Anger* (Rider, 2005) Mark Fisher writes:

> There are four causes of anger:
>
> 1   Failure to achieve a personal goal, for example arriving late for a meeting; failing an exam; losing a job.

2   Invasion of a personal boundary – for example someone entering a room or personal space without permission: being touched without permission; being spoken to disrespectfully.

3   Self-defence anger – for example feeling the constant need to defend yourself because you are not intelligent enough to do your job.

4   Shadow projection – you are embarrassed about your working-class origins and try to conceal them.

Fisher speaks of 'Imploders' and 'Exploders'.

Imploders swallow their anger. They bottle it up for long periods of time, for reasons of fear, insecurity and low self-esteem. Imploders are terrified of both their own and other peoples anger and fear, rejection and abandonment.

The people most at risk of stress are those who bottle their anger up and never get rid of it. The negative energy of their anger is trapped and held in the body. The body acts like a pressure cooker. The anger builds and builds until one day the valve blows and the anger comes streaming out; more often than not in the form of full-blown rage.

Anger has consequences. If we are aggressive we need to become aware of the effects of our outbursts. When we allow our anger to explode, however, we never need to consider what is at stake. Not only will we do and say things which we later regret but we also make ourselves a target for all sorts of abuse from others, and even run the risk of becoming a scapegoat.

A legitimate question is whether Wallace, in this light of his endless denials of guilt, may have suffered from post-traumatic amnesia. This is defined in the *Penguin Dictionary of Psychology* as 'any loss of memory following traumatic experience. Traumatic here may be used to describe either a physical injury or a disturbing psychological experience'.

David Canter, the well known exponent of the science of criminal profiling makes a significant point in his book *Criminal Shadows* (Harper Collins, 1995) which may well be relevant to the Wallace case:

A man who plans his life and thinks things through, who holds down a job which makes some demands on his manual or intellectual skills, will go about the business of murder, rather differently from the casual, confused ne'er do well. An organised crime scene will be produced by an organised criminal. The person who leaves his victim in a hurry with no attempt at concealment is likely to have left many difficult situations in his life in a hurry and be known for his haphazard ways.

What we know about Wallace is that he certainly fits the description of an 'Imploder' and undoubtedly was a well organised man.

Yet all this, while providing an interesting field of speculation carries the case of murder against Wallace no further whatever.

CHAPTER TWELVE

RICHARD GORDON PARRY

From the date of Wallace's trial only one name has been advanced, by those who believe in Wallace's innocence, as the real murderer. That is the name of Richard Gordon Parry. At the conclusion of his writings for publication Wallace says this:

> Only now do I know that at the time of the crime he was in desperate straights. And I have found that he had been convicted of offences involving money. Today a report reaches me that his appearance suggests mental disturbance and deterioration.

> I have no doubt whatever in my mind that he [Parry] was the man who murdered my poor wife. I think with horror at the very thought of the brutality he displayed.... If I had ever reason to seek the death of my wife I could not have used such methods as those by which she died. I have been a teacher of Science and Chemistry, and at the time of the tragedy I had at my command, even in my house, materials by which with a score of methods her end could have been brought about painlessly and without attracting suspicion.

> If I were to die tomorrow I would have only one wish – to see the murderer brought to justice and this terrible stigma removed from me. Revenge will not bring my dear wife back again, but I shall be satisfied if justice is done .

In the trial of Wallace the prosecution has been criticised for shifting its ground on the suggested theory of how the murder was committed. It is however noteworthy that the defence contented itself with disputing the evidence advanced by the Crown and never put before the jury a convincing alternative explanation. This is apparent from Oliver's closing speech to the jury:

> Now, members of the jury, take some of the things which were put to him [Wallace] in cross-examination and see how frank he was. It was put to him by my learned friend the Recorder, that, when the telephoning took place on January 19th, that would have been a splendid opportunity, would it not, to have gone and robbed your house when you were known to be at the chess club? That may be argued again. He frankly said it would have been. But members of the jury do not forget the argument against it. He is not arguing his case you know; he is just answering the questions. The arguments against it keep in mind. They could not know if they saw him go out, and were watching him, that he was going to the chess club. [Here Oliver is making a point for the prosecution, which is that the mysterious caller must have known Wallace was going to the club.] They might think he might go there, and being the ordinary pay day of the Prudential it is said that is the most likely day to get a good haul. That is the answer, not given by him, but mere

argument coming from me; and I ask you to weigh it. Then the next thing put to him is this: you had two doors to this place and there must have been two watchers, is that an insuperable difficulty? Do you think that is unlikely? Do these sort of people, if they did this never work in pairs?

What did Oliver mean by 'these sort of people?' It is said that Mr Justice Wright directed that the name of Parry should not be disclosed at the trial, but the fact remains that Oliver never put forward a convincing suspect to the jury.

Richard Gordon Parry was a young man of 22 at the time of Julia Wallace's murder. He was well known to Wallace as they had been colleagues in the Prudential Insurance Company. They had met on several occasions at the City Café because Parry was a member of an amateur dramatic society which, like the chess club to which Wallace belonged, used the cafe for it's meetings. This meant that Parry would have been in a position to see the fixtures for matches at the chess club, including those for which Wallace was due to attend. Furthermore Parry visited the Wallace home, and on at least one occasion took over Wallace's 'round' when Wallace was unwell. Parry liked to sing and, on his own (much later) admission, sometimes joined Julia for a musical evening when Wallace was out and was not aware of the presence of Parry in his home.

Wallace refers to Parry in his statement to the police dated 22 January 1931:

> Mr Gordon R Parry of Derwent Road, Stoneycroft, is a friend of my late wife and myself. He is now an agent for the Gresham Insurance Company. But I am not sure of the company. He was employed by the Prudential up to about twelve or fifteen months ago, and he then resigned to improve his position. Although nothing was known officially to the company detrimental to his financial affairs, it was known that he had collected premiums which he did not pay in and his superintendent Mr Crewe, of Green Lane, Allerton, told me that he went to Parry's parents who paid about £30 to cover the deficiency. Mr Crewe's office is at 2, Great Nelson Street. Parry is a single man about 22 years of age. I have known him about three years and he was with my company about two years. I was ill with bronchitis in December 1928 and Parry did part of my collecting for about two or three days a week for about three weeks. I discovered slight discrepancies and I spoke to him about it. He was short of small amounts when paying in, and he had entered all the amounts collected in the book. When I spoke to him he said it was an oversight and that he was sorry and that he would put the matter right.

> Previous to Parry doing my work he had called at my home once on business and had left a letter for me which he wrote in my front room. I was not in at the time but my wife let him in. While he was doing my work on the 29th December he called very frequently to see me about business, and he was well

acquainted with our domestic arrangements. He had been in the parlour and the kitchen frequently and had been upstairs in the middle bedroom a number of times to see me while I was in bed, I do not think he called to see me after I resumed work in January 1929, but if he had called my wife would have had no hesitation in admitting him. I have often seen him since he has been working for his new company and have spoken to him. About last November I was in the City Café one evening, I think it was on a Thursday, playing chess and I saw Parry there. He was not playing chess. He was by himself walking across the room. I said Good evening and he returned my greeting. I think that was the last time I saw him. He is a member of an amateur dramatic society which holds its meeting at the City Café on Thursday evenings. I do not think he drinks. He is engaged to a Miss Lloyd, 7 Missourie Road, Clubmoor. He would be on a weekly salary from his company plus commission on business and his earnings would be about £4 a week.

There was another man named Marsden who also did part of the work for me while I was ill in December 1928. I do not know his address. He was an agent for the Prudential Company for two or three years and had left before he did my work. I gave him the job because he was out of work. Parry recommended him. I have heard that Parry left the Prudential on account of financial irregularities. While he was working for me he often came to my house to see me on business. He also knew the interior arrangements of my house, I have seen Marsden several times since he worked for me, I do not know if he is working now and I do not know anything about his private affairs. If he had called at my house my wife would have asked him in. Both Parry and Marsden knew the arrangements of my business with regard to the system of paying in money collected to the Head Office, Dale Street. There is a definite order of the Company's that money must be paid in on Wednesdays, but this is not strictly enforced and I paid it in on Thursdays usually, I have had the cash-box from which the money was stolen for about 16 years, I always put the Company's money in that box and it was always kept on top of the bookcase in the kitchen during the day time. At night I always took it upstairs to my bedroom, Parry and Marsden knew I kept the money in the box because while they worked for me I always put the money into it when they called to pay over to me their collections. They had both seen me take it down and put it back to the top of the bookcase in the kitchen often.

Marsden is about 28 years of age, about 5 foot 6/7 inches, brown hair, and fairly well dressed. Parry is about 5 foot 10 inches, slimmish build, and dark hair, rather foppish appearance, well dressed and wears spats, very plausible.

Superintendent Crowe, his assistant Mr Wood, 26 Ellersley Road, Mr J Bamber, assistant superintendent, 48 Kingsfield Road, Orral Park, employees of the company, would be admitted by my wife without hesitation if they called. They are Mr F W Jenkinson, his son Frederick, 29 years, his daughter 16 and his wife. They live at 116 Moscow Drive. Mr James Caird, 3 Letchworth Street Anfield, his wife and family. He has two grown up sons. Mr Davis the music teacher of Queens Drive, Walton who is teaching me the violin. Mr Hayes my tailor of Breck Road.

I forgot to mention that I believe Mr Parry owns a motor car or has the use of one, because I was talking to him about Christmas time in Missouri Road and he had a car then which he was driving. He gave me one of his company's calendars.

This statement, which is clearly intended to cast suspicion on Parry and Marsden, was made at a time when Wallace obviously realised that as the husband of Julia, he must be a suspect himself. Yet Wallace told the police at the time of handing to them the above names that he did not suspect any of them of having murdered his wife; a statement he repeated at his trial.

How strong is the case against Parry? Roger Wilkes in his book *Wallace, the Final Verdict* lists eight points which he submits, add up to a damaging case against Parry.

1. He had two motives, one for simple robbery, to avenge Wallace's treachery in reporting his accountancy discrepancies. And a second for murder, to silence the sole witness of his bungled attempt at theft. Wallace claimed that Parry was hard up at the time of the killing.

2. He had the means; the ability as an amateur actor, to have disguised his voice convincingly during the telephone call; the use of a car to get to and from Wolverton Street; and access to a murder weapon, either something to hand in the house, or an implement he took there himself.

3. He had opportunity; he knew where Wallace's insurance takings were kept; was virtually assured of being admitted to the house by Mrs Wallace, and knew that Wallace himself would be out of the way long enough to commit robbery without risk of interruption.

4. After the killing, Parry claimed at least three different alibis, the first (reportedly to the police) that he had spent the evening with friends, one of whom Lily Lloyd, he named, the second (to his father) that he was fixing his car in Breck Road; the third (to Goodman and Whittingston-Egan) that he had been arranging a birthday celebration with friends.

5. Parry, named to the police by Wallace, was evidently the strongest initial suspect.

6. His antecedents, a history of pilfering, car stealing and his alleged violent nature, weigh against him.

7. Lily Lloyd stands by her 1933 version of events, admitting that Parry did not join her until late on the murder night, late enough to deprive Parry of an alibi, for the time of the killing.

8. The substantial new evidence of John Parkes concerning Parry's visit to Atkinson garage, recounted for no reward or inducement other than 'to get it off my mind after all these years'.

How valid are these various points.

1. The fundamental weakness of the argument for Parry being the killer is that the purpose of Qualtrough, whoever he was, was homicide not theft. The view taken by the police, that the signs of disturbance in the house were an attempt by the killer to create a false impression that the murder had been committed in the course of a burglary was clearly an opinion shared by the court of trial. Indeed Oliver never tried to argue otherwise. He confined himself to blocking the points against Wallace. Why on earth should Parry, having only found £4 in the money box resort to such a terrible method of escaping detection so as to rain blows on the head of Julia, beating her brains out. In any event we know that more valuable items were left untouched.

As for the allegation of an act of vengeance the fact is that Parry had no cause for a grudge against Wallace. He left the Prudential of his own accord and immediately found employment with the Gresham Insurance Company. After his change of work Parry showed no hostility towards Wallace on the occasions when the two met. In any event, why vent his wrath on poor, innocent Julia and not on Wallace himself. Parry had comfortably off parents who had helped him out financially on several occasions. With such a source available would he really murder for a few pounds.

2. As to the telephone call this has been dealt with in an earlier chapter. Was Parry hanging about outside 29 Wolverton Street without any certainty that Wallace would be leaving the house, let alone going to the chess club. The call was made at 7.15pm. the very time when Wallace would have been able to reach the kiosk. How did Parry follow Wallace along Richmond Park without being spotted? By the time he reached the telephone kiosk Wallace would have been along Breck Road and turning into Belmont Road, and still Parry would have no certainty that he was going to the chess club.

As to the use of a car in connection with the murder and access to the weapon these are matters of pure conjecture.

3. Parry would have had no reason to know that Wallace would be out of the way long enough to suit his purpose. Wallace might well have been

put on his guard by the mysterious message and have returned home after a short interval. In any event Parry was familiar with Wallace's absences from his home as an insurance agent and would have had no cause to send him off on a 'wild goose chase'. Of course Parry knew where the takings were kept and would have been admitted to the house by Julia. But this was also true of other people.

4.   Those who wished to implicate Parry have always pointed to the fact that Lily Lloyd, who gave him the initial alibi to the police, later, after he had jilted her, told Munro, Wallace's solicitor, that she wished to withdraw her previous statement, and that Parry had only been with her for the late part of the evening. Munro declined to act upon this, he may well have taken the view that this was simply the result of a woman scorned taking revenge. Any statement made in such circumstances had to be unreliable

James Murphy writing in his book *The Murder of Julia Wallace*, quotes the Parry's statement to the police on Friday 23 January:

On Tuesday 20th I finished business about 5.30pm and called upon Mr Brine 43 Knocklaid Road. I remained there with Mrs Brine, her daughter Savona 13 years, and her nephew Harold Denison, 29 Marlborough Road, until about 8.30pm. I then went out and bought some cigarettes – Players No 3, and the evening express from Mr Hodgson's post office, Maiden Lane, on the way to my young lady's house. When I was turning the corner by the post office I remembered that I had promised to call for my accumulator at Hignetts in West Derby Road, Tuebrook. I went there and got my accumulator and then went down West Derby Road and along Lisburn Lane to Mrs Williamson 49 Lisburn Lane, and saw her. We had a chat about a 21st Birthday party for about ten minutes and then I went to 7 Missouri Road, and remained there till about 11 to 11.30 when I went home.

I have heard of the murder of Mrs Wallace and have studied the newspaper reports of the case and naturally being acquainted with Mr and Mrs Wallace, I have taken a great interest in it, I have no objection whatsoever to the police verifying my statements as to my movements at the 19th and the 20th instant.

The statement of Mrs Olivia Brine is as follows:

I am a married woman; my husband is away at sea. I have known R G Parry for about two years. Just before last Christmas he commenced calling with my nephew William Dennison, 29 Marlborough Road, at about 5pm to 5.30pm on Tuesday 20th inst, Parry called at my house. He came in his car; he remained until about 8.30pm when he left. Whilst he was here, a Miss Plant, Gloucester Road, called. My nephew, Harold Dennison, also called.

These times were corroborated by Harold English Dennison.

John Sharpe Johnston, Wallace's neighbour, gave evidence that he and his wife were leaving their house at about a quarter to nine when Wallace arrived home, Parry's movements were checked by the police and he was eliminated from the enquiry.

Wallace's statement in court bears repetition in the light of his later imputations regarding Parry:

HEMMERDE: Although you gave certain names to the police of persons she might have admitted, is there one of them against whom you have the slightest suspicion of having committed this offence?

WALLACE: No.

5.   The police cleared Parry after exhaustive investigations.

6.   The criminal record of Parry has been greatly exaggerated by the pro-Wallace writers. In fact, by today's standards, it was fairly mild. At the time of the Wallace trial it consisted of a few minor offences involving dishonesty regarding small sums of money. Much later he was convicted of theft of a car and indecent assault. If small offenders progress to greater crimes then there was no sign of this in the 22 year old Parry.

7.   Parry does not depend on Lily Lloyd for his alibi.

8.   It was just before Radio City's Broadcast in 1981 'Who Killed Julia Wallace' that a message was received by Roger Wilkes and Michael Green that someone living had cleaned Parry's car on the night of the murder. This person was John Parkes who on the night of the 20 January 1931, was working at Atkinson's Garage in the vicinity of the Wallace's home. What he had to say was quite extraordinary. Parry arrived in his car after 11pm and requested Parkes to hose it both inside and out. Parkes picked up a glove from the glove compartment which he said was stained with blood, Parry seized the glove with words to the effect of 'if the police found this glove it would hang me'. Parry according to Parkes then spoke about a metal bar he had pushed down a drain. Atkinson, the owner of the garage told Parkes to say nothing about it, when Wallace was convicted they did contact the police. Superintendent Moore listened to the story but dismissed it as a mistake.

This statement of Parkes, if presented as fresh evidence which had not been available at the trial, could have been crucial at Wallace's appeal. It never was. How reliable was Parkes?

First of all it must be borne in mind that this was the recollection of an old man about something which was alleged to have happened a whole half century earlier. There is no record of Parkes alleged interview with Moore and no corroboration of Parkes story. In 1981 Atkinson was dead and could provide no confirmation. If, as is presumed to be the case, Parry wore the glove when killing Julia, why did he not dispose of it instead of carrying it around in his car at a time when the police investigations were in full swing. All the drains in the area were searched but no iron bar was found.

The argument for Parry's guilt enters the realms of farce in the suggestion that Parry avoided blood stains on his clothing by obtaining a set of fishermans' waterproofs and was wearing these when he called at 29 Wolverton Street for the purpose of murdering Julia Wallace. Furthermore, would Parry take his car to a garage where he was well known and make admissions of murder, which he would realise might well be reported to the police who were hunting everywhere for clues. Parkes said Parry was with another man – but why should he heighten the risk of detection by involving another person.

The fact is that the case against Parry is dubious to say the least. Since he is the only real alternative suspect that leaves one person in the frame – William Herbert Wallace.

CHAPTER THIRTEEN

THE SOLUTION

It is perhaps a bold gesture, in a case as puzzling as the Wallace case, to offer a solution. This is particularly so when many writers and criminologists of distinction have had such difficulty in finding the answer. Yet behind the mystery, the lack of any direct evidence and the differing interpretations of the known facts, there has to be an answer. Can we find it? Expressions like 'the perfect crime' and 'the motiveless murder' are not very helpful. They discourage any attempt to discover the truth. They also dispute the fact that there is no such thing as a perfect crime. There is merely the crime in which the vital clue has never been found. Moreover, the only motiveless murders are those committed by psychopathic killers seized by a blood-lust such as is the case with the majority of serial homicidal maniacs.

The second point to make is that 'domestic' murders really are in a different category from most others. They can be, as in the case of Armstrong, motivated by greed, but this is only rarely so. Far more often the crime has an emotional base; revenge at an injury suffered, such as infidelity or ill treatment, or the result of a desire to escape from a intolerable situation. Even in this day and age, when divorce is a far easier option than it used to be years ago, violence in marriage, even murder, is sadly not uncommon.

We shall take a closer of the Wallace marriage later in this chapter, but first let us take another look at the known facts. It is not the intention of this author to review this case again in any detail. The arguments both for and against William Wallace are already familiar to the reader.

The two key features of the trial were these: first, who made the telephone call? In other words who was Qualtrough? The second is: Was Wallace's search for 25 Menlove Gardens East the result of a bogus message which he had sent to himself to provide an alibi for the murder of his wife? Or had he been genuinely misled by the real murderer to get him out of the way at the time when the crime was committed? These are the two issues of crucial importance.

First let us take the situation regarding the telephone box. At the trial it is very noticeable that Roland Oliver took his client swiftly through his movements on his journey to the chess club on the evening of the 19 January:

OLIVER: We know you were due to go and play a match of chess. I will take this as shortly as I can. What time did you leave your house to go to the chess club?

WALLACE: As near as I can tell you, about a quarter past seven.

OLIVER: That is the time you gave to the police near the event?

WALLACE: Yes.

OLIVER: How did you go there. By what method? I do not want the whole route [the jury might have done], but did you walk or go by tram or how?

WALLACE: I walked up Richmond Park, turned the corner by the church and up Belmont Road, and there caught a tram.

OLIVER: It has been suggested that you used the telephone box to telephone a message to yourself, is there a word of truth in that?

WALLACE: Absolutely none.

Defenders of Wallace who maintain that he would not have had the time to make the phone call and reach the chess club when he was seen there overlook one very important fact. Wallace's evidence regarding the time he left home, the route he took and the time and place at which he boarded the tram to the club is completely uncorroborated. However, on his own evidence if he left home at around 7.15 his walk along Richmond Road would, had he turned right and not left at the church corner, have brought him to the kiosk at the precise time that 'Qualtrough' was making the call. Is this one coincidence too many?

The technical fault on the line is something the caller could not have expected. Evidence of this was given at the trial by the telephone engineer Leslie Heaton. The caller had to be put through because, due to the fault, he had pressed button B to retrieve his money. This was the reason that the call was logged and the number of the call box was recorded. On such unforeseen events are the cleverest of criminals sometimes caught.

Wallace agreed that his route took him within easy reach of the telephone kiosk. He might well have taken a tram, or indeed a bus, from near the kiosk which could well have got him to the chess club by the time he was seen there by James Caird. If he was catching a conveyance in Belmont Road he was following a roundabout route. To walk down Castlewood Road, the way he returned after leaving the chess club later that evening, would have been much quicker. As to the question of a disguised voice, that would create no serious difficulty. In 1931 the reception on a telephone line was much inferior to today. A change to a more powerful, forceful voice could certainly deceive the listener. There would be no need to impersonate a foreign accent.

148

The second issue, the search for 25 Menlove Gardens East; was it genuine or not? This was dealt with fairly briefly by Mr Justice Wright in his summing up:

> The learned Recorder pointed out, and pointed out with considerable force, that it was very foolish of him [Wallace] to go on like that, that he might have taken steps through his friends to see whether there was Mr Qualtrough, or to see whether there was a 25 Menlove Gardens East, and when he got there, and everybody told him there was no such place as Menlove Gardens East, it was very foolish of him to go on making enquiries, and he ought to have gone home at once and given it up as a bad job.

> There was a great deal of force in that; and the learned Recorder pointed out, that if this was an alibi two things would be natural; first that he should speak to his friends, as many as possible and in such a way as would impress upon them that he was there at that time; and that he should tell the police as soon as the crime was discovered what he had been doing so that they could help him establish his alibi. Of course that is a possible view, and you have to consider that. But it is one aspect of the case, and there is another view. If the prisoner had not committed the crime, and had not sent the telephone message; if he was going quite honestly to search for Mr Qualtrough in Menlove Gardens East in the hope of getting a useful commission – as it is a lucrative business, new insurance – then no doubt, having gone so far and having told his wife, as he says he did, all about it he would anyhow not have gone home but have probed the matter to the bottom. It may be that he was very foolish, but on the other hand it is very difficult to say that his doing so points to his having committed the crime.

Many years later, we recall, Mr Justice Wright, now Lord Wright of Durley, expressed a private view:

> Never forget that Wallace was a chess player... I should say that broadly speaking, any man with common sense would have said that Wallace's alibi was too good to be true, but that is not an argument you can hang a man on.

If Wallace is the culprit there are two questions to be asked: Firstly, how did he do it? And secondly why did he do it? In his book *The Killing of Julia Wallace*, Jonathan Goodman cites five points which he maintains, somewhat boldly this author suggests, prove conclusively that Wallace was innocent. With respect to that very able and interesting writer – they prove no such thing. The seven points made by Goodman concern the following:

1. Wallace's demeanour and his remarks on the night of the murder.

2. Wallace's persistence in trying to locate 25 Menlove Gardens East.

3. The apparent absence of motive.

4. The telephone call.

5. The alleged alibi.

6. The murder weapon.

7. If Wallace didn't do it – who did?

Let us take each of these points:

1. The equivocal nature of Wallace's demeanour:

On the subject of the demeanour of Wallace at the murder scene Goodman is on strong ground. Certainly his reaction is wholly different from what one might expect from a great many other people; but by no stretch of imagination can this be regarded as an item of circumstantial evidence.

2. The sincerity of Wallace's search:

Neither of the two examples Goodman gives in the course of his own experience is truly analogous to the Wallace search. In the former case, Goodman was looking for an address which did in fact exist. The policeman he spoke to in fact gave him correct directions and at no time said that there was no such place as Belgrave Gardens North! In the second example, Belgrave Mews East was non-existent, but although Goodman's friend made several enquiries we are not told whether he was told by two people, one of whom was a police officer, at an early stage, that there was no such place.

Wallace's persistence in looking for Menlove Gardens East can be argued both ways. It is certainly makes no contribution to proving his innocence.

3. The apparent absence of motive does not prove that no motive exists:

The absence of an obvious or clear motive was emphasised by Mr Justice Wright in his summing up:

> Now when we come to consider the evidence here on the question of motive, I do not think I can say anything at all. All the evidence is that the prisoner and his wife, to all appearances were living together in happiness and amity. You have heard the evidence. There was no pecuniary inducement that one can see for the prisoner to desire the death of his wife: She had a small insurance policy in her life, a matter of £20, and she had something like £90 in the savings bank. But there is no reason to think that he wanted that £20, for if he did want it, he could have got it because he had a bank balance of his own. There was nothing that he could gain, so far as one can see, by her death.

Goodman is right to question the suggestion that Wallace's kidney ailment was the cause of a mental breakdown that may have triggered the murder. Nor does a degree of boastfulness in Wallace's writing amount to anything of importance. But motive? The words of Mr Justice Wright in 1964 are instructive:

> So may strange things happen in life, I should not and never did, demand a motive for any crime? Very often the only motive is merely impulse, and you must remember that Wallace was a highly strung man. But if Wallace did murder his wife, as the jury thought, there might have been a motive.... After the trial the station master at Birkenhead Station mentioned the case to me as I waited for a train. He said it was the opinion of people in the district that there was another woman in the case. That certainly never came out at the trial. But at the time I could not help thinking that Wallace found domestic felicity a little boring, as it is apt to be occasionally to anybody.

Some domestic murders are motivated by material considerations – but many are not. In the case of the majority the reason behind it is revenge. As I write these words I have before me a report in the newspaper of a woman who was convicted of the murder of her husband by repeated blows to his head with a hammer. The reason was her fury over his constant affairs with other women. On arrest her comment was: 'If I can't have him nobody else will'. We shall consider this aspect later in the this chapter.

4.   The telephone call has already been discussed in this work. It would not, as Goodman suggests, be impossible for Wallace to disguise his voice, nor would the poorly lit kiosk be an unsuitable place for Wallace to make his call. Caird was not precise about the time at which Wallace arrived at the chess club, and as James Murphy points out in *The Murder of Julia Wallace* buses as well as trams were available for the journey.

5.   The Oxford English Dictionary defines alibi as:

> A claim or piece of evidence that one was elsewhere when an alleged act took place.

Wallace said that he left home on the evening of the 20 January at 6.45pm. After his search for 25 Menlove Gardens he arrived home at 8.45pm (seen by the Johnstons). During that period of two hours (Close says he saw Julia alive at 6.30pm) Julia Wallace was murdered. If Wallace created the Qualtrough story he was successful, for defenders of Wallace have always maintained that between Close calling at the house and Wallace's departure there was not enough time for Wallace to commit the murder and complete all the other arrangements that were necessary to cleanse himself of blood and create the impression that a burglary had taken place. The experienced criminologist and writer Nigel Morland, in his book *Background to Murder* (Werner Laurie, 1955) maintains that there was ample time and that his own experimentation of what he believes happened confirm this. Moreover,

Qualtrough would have had to enter the house within a very short time of Wallace's departure. Call it an alibi or not it was the 'Qualtrough' story which enabled Wallace to escape execution.

6. The iron bar is one of the many mysteries attached to the Wallace case. Its presence in the parlour before the murder and its subsequent disappearance carries the case no further either for Wallace or against him. All that is certain is that after an exhaustive police search it was never found.

7. If Wallace didn't do it, who did? Let us now review those points of which we can be certain.

Firstly, the telephone call was made from a kiosk which was a mere five minutes walk, if as much, from Wallace's house.

Secondly, the identity of the kiosk might never have been discovered.

Thirdly, the call was made at a time when Wallace could have been in the kiosk.

Fourthly, the caller knew that Wallace was an insurance agent; how strange says Morland that he knew so much about Wallace but Wallace, apparently knew so little about him.

Fifthly, Wallace's repeated requests for information were sufficient to at least arouse suspicion that he wanted to establish the fact of his search.

Now once more, Mr Justice Wright's direction to the jury:

> The question is not who did this crime? The question is: did the prisoner do it? – or rather to put it more accurately: Is it proved to your reasonable satisfaction and beyond all reasonable doubt that the prisoner did it? It is a fallacy to say: If the prisoner did not do it, who did?

The Judge's summing up on that central issue is impeccable. Nevertheless, in deciding the central issue of 'did the prisoner do it', it is surely a reasonable and acceptable course to ask the question – who are the alternative suspects? Can they be eliminated? Again, one can surely draw the analogy of the medical practitioner who applies a number of tests to exclude other possible causes of the symptoms in order to isolate, and therefore identify, the true source of the disease.

There were no signs of a breaking into 29 Wolverton Street. Nor were there any indications that a struggle had taken place. This must exclude an unknown criminal, who in any event would be ignorant of Wallace's profession. There had been burglaries in the neighbourhood, but none

152

accompanied by violence; hence it must follow that the murderer was either the occupant of the house or a person who Julia Wallace had admitted. Among those who Mrs Wallace would have admitted, defenders of Wallace have pointed the finger of guilt at one person only: Richard Gordon Parry. If there is any serious doubt about his involvement – and I have suggested in the previous chapter why there is serious doubt, that leaves only Wallace himself.

There are several pieces of evidence which, although brushed aside at the trial, may still be worthy of consideration. Lily Hall was a poor witness as to times and directions, but there is little doubt that she was being truthful. She made her statement a week after the event, but was ill during that time and her testimony was given to the police at her bedside. She claimed to have seen Wallace on the night of the 20 January at 8.35pm at the bottom of the entry to Richmond Park. He was taking to another man. She said that she saw them quite clearly from the light given by a street lamp further along the road, She said the two men parted, going different ways. Miss Hall said that although she had not met Wallace, she and her mother had frequently spoken to Mrs Wallace after church service and she knew Wallace well by sight. If this evidence was true, it meant that Wallace was lying when he said he had not spoken to anyone on his way home after his search for 25 Menlove Gardens East. It also ran counter to his evidence that he hurried home on that occasion.

Mr Justice Wright dealt with the matter very briefly:

Then you come back to Wolverton Street, and there is the evidence of Miss Lily Hall, no doubt saying what she thinks she saw. She thinks she saw the prisoner at 8.35. And you have heard from the prosecution what importance, such as it is, they attach to that. The prisoner says he was not there, and it is word against word. It was night, and there is no special reason apparently, why Miss Hall should have made all these observations, or even with regard to the time, that she should be accurate. Therefore I put that aside, and you will give such weight to it as you think right. What is significant is the fact that Lily identified Wallace without hesitation at an identity parade held by the police.

The evidence of police constable James Rothwell received little attention – probably a good deal less that it should have done. It will be recalled that Rothwell passed Wallace at about 3.30pm in Maiden Lane on 20th January. He described Wallace as 'Haggard and drawn, and he was very distressed – unusually distressed'.

He was dabbing his eye with his coat – sleeve and he appeared to me as if he had been crying. I have never seen him like that before.

Rothwell was an experienced officer, he knew Wallace well by sight and he passed quite close to him. He did not agree that Wallace may have been rubbing his eyes because they were watering due to the cold, nor did he accept that he might be mistaken because there were other witnesses who had seen Wallace after that time who would say he appeared perfectly normal to them.

It must be remembered that Wallace had an extraordinary gift of control over his emotions, and the appearance of the police officer may well have had this effect. If it may be that Rothwell's observation was correct, it raises the question of what was the cause of Wallace's grief. It would have had to be connected with his relationship with his wife. Yet Wallace maintained that when he had tea later that day with Julia everything was normal.

One of the main points always made in favour of Wallace's innocence is the time factor. At the most Wallace would have had between 6.30pm and 6.50pm to commit the murder and create the impression of a burglary, and also to clean any bloodstains from his clothing and his person. As Mr Justice Wright said in his summing up, 'the murderer must have worked with lightning rapidity and effectiveness'.

However it must be remembered that this was a crime planned well in advance with every eventuality having been taken into consideration. The lay-out of the parlour, as appears from a photograph of the murder scene, shows the piano open with a music score in place. May it not have been the situation that while Julia was preoccupied with playing the piano Wallace carried out some of the changes required to give the bogus impression of a burglary.

In 1932 Wallace wrote his 'life story' which was serialised in *John Bull Magazine*. In this he attempts to reconstruct the crime: To reiterate.

He followed my wife into the sitting room, and as she bent down and lit the gas-fire he struck her, possibly with a spanner. The implement of murder was never discovered. Now he had to kill her. To strike her again while she lay on the floor and him standing over her would mean the upward spurting of blood. Two strides took him into the lobby, where he had observed my mackintosh hanging, and he held it as a shield between him and her body while he bludgeoned her to death. She must have been felled as soon as she lit the fire and before she could regulate the flow of gas. It would have been at full blaze and as he bent at the fireplace the flames set alight the mackintosh.

Then he would see that the bottom edge of her skirt was burning, and, throwing the mackintosh down, he must have dragged her away from the fire an onto part of the coat, leaving her in the position I found her.

Wallace might have added, that had the killer been kneeling down when he delivered the remaining ten blows which were responsible for most of the blood, and holding out the mackintosh on his left forearm in the style of a matador, this would have meant that his body was effectively protected from the blood.

Was this theory, which differs somewhat from those advanced at the trial, a genuine reproduction from Wallace's imagination, or was it Wallace's own recollection of what he himself had done?

A sixth point was made by the great writer of crime stories, Raymond Chandler: 'How strange that Qualtrough knew so much about Wallace, but Wallace apparently knew nothing at all about Qualtrough'.

In his book *Wallace: The Final Verdict* Roger Wilkes refers to a remarkable incident which never found it's way into the trial. Next door to the Wallace's lived Mr and Mrs Holme at number 27. Mr Holme arrived back from work at 6.30pm, and while he and his wife were having tea in the kitchen a noise was heard which attracted their attention. Mrs Holme asked her husband if someone was at their front door, Mr Holme replied that the sound came from the Wallace's. Mrs Holme stated that it was like the sound of someone falling – shortly afterwards the front door of 29 was heard to close. Since it would have taken a few minutes for the Holmes to settle down to tea these times may be less than accurate. The sound of a falling body is distinct and the walls of the houses in Wolverton Street were thin. Certainly this disturbance was heard at a time when Wallace was still on the premises. Did perhaps Wallace leave by the front door at some time between 6.30pm and 6.50pm, and is that the reason why he gave differing accounts regarding the circumstance of his departure from the back door?

We have considered the 'how' of Wallace having murdered his wife, now it is time to investigate the 'why'.

It is difficult to accept, without a fair degree of doubt, Wallace's description of his marriage as one unbroken story of idyllic happiness and undisturbed peace. Even if one discounts the statements of Mrs Wilson and Dr Curwen, which paint a very different picture, to accept all that Wallace wrote in his diary would seem a little naïve. As Lord Wright said of Wallace's alibi, so also it may be said of his accounts of his and Julia's domestic bliss as 'too good to be true'. Mrs Wilson who nursed Wallace through a bout of pneumonia, like Dr Curwen, had seen the Wallace's marriage from the inside; theirs was not the impression given to outsiders who encountered the pair when they were on their best behaviour towards each other. Many a marriage which is less than happy maintains a facade of a peaceful relationship which is not the true story.

Raymond Chandler writing in 1951 said of the diary which Wallace kept:

> I feel that with a man of Wallace's type a diary is the only outlet, and as a very occasional diarist I also feel that the moment a man sets his thoughts down on paper, however secretly, he is in a sense writing for publication … There is nothing quoted from Wallace's diary after the trial... which I could not imagine a man writing in the circumstances. There is such a thing as remorse; there is such a thing as the wish to believe that the irreversible never happened. Wallace has posed to himself as a stoic; in his behaviour after the murder there is something more than pose. In his diary he clings to the last shred of pride he has – his pride in this stoical behaviour, the last stability of a ruined life.

There is little doubt that Julia Wallace should and could have done better than to marry William. There is something in his constant re-iteration of their alleged ecstatic relationship which does not ring quite true, The change from the life Julia had in her earlier years, living in the pleasant villa at 11 St Mary's Avenue, Harrogate, compared with the dingy 'up and down' in a dreary working class area of Liverpool must have been very great, There was far less social mobility in the 1930s than there is today, and if a woman married down she was trapped in the life style which her husband gave her. Wallace, notwithstanding his fantasising about himself and his supposed intellectual gifts, was a failure and he must have felt the inner humiliation of his inability to give his cultured and better educated wife the standard of living she deserved. He compensated for this by persuading himself and others that, nevertheless, he was making her happy.

Yseult Bridges, in her book *Two Studies in Crime* gives a compelling account of the drabness of Julia's surroundings and the dreariness of her existence:

> From her bedroom window the only view she could command was of a chequer board of backyards extending on either hand, and on both sides of a central alley. Each one the repository of battered dustbins and the site of ramshackle coal sheds. Here not even a stunted tree put out a hopeful leaf in spring, and the only colour to regale Julia's eye was provided by the washing flapping from the clothes-lines every Monday.

> How stultifying that background! How different to the one that had been hers at 11 St Mary's Avenue with it's wide windows, pleasant little garden and trim surrounding!

As to Julia's own personal circumstances Yseult Bridges writes:

In all those sixteen years of existence in Wolverton Street fashions underwent may changes,. But, winter and summer, Julia continued to wear three dresses with long, flared skirts and hems almost touching the ground, which had been the vogue at the time of her marriage. Such a one was she wearing when she was murdered, and after it had been removed at the mortuary her undercloth-ing was found to be in a pitiable state. This had been awkwardly contrived by herself out of the cheapest material, and was clumsily darned and patched, for she did not number sewing among her accomplishments. It was then too, that the pathetic little hoard of some thirty shillings was discovered stitched into her ragged corsets. But more pathetic still was the emaciated condition of her body, bearing as it did all the signs of chronic under nourishment. At fifty-two though suffering from no disease, she had become a feeble, weak, woman to quote the evidence of Professor MacFall. It was into this scenario that there entered Richard Gordon Parry. Parry who we have seen in the pre-vious chapter had become a fellow employee of Wallace in the Prudential, became a frequent visitor to the Wallace home. He took over Wallace's work on one occasion when the latter was ill and the two met both before and after the murder. Wallace, who had named Parry to the police as one of a number of persons to whom Julia would have granted admission to 20 Wolverton Street finally, accused him of being the murderer in an article published in John Bull Magazine.

Parry was a handsome young man who liked the good life but lacked the wherewithal to support it. He enjoyed music, theatre, wine and, noteably, women. This included married women of mature years. His frequent visits to Mrs Brine whose husband was away at sea, would indicate this. But most importantly, from the point of view of the mystery of the murder, was the attention he undoubtedly paid to Julia Wallace. Parry was well acquainted with William's work routine and with his absences from home – when they occurred and how long they lasted. In an interview, on the 30 March 1966, with Jonathan Goodman, Parry admitted that he and Julia enjoyed musical afternoons together, he singing and Julia playing the piano. The significance of these is not their occurrence, but the fact that Wallace was kept in ignorance of them. Since Parry belonged to an amateur dramatic society which met at the City Café, the same location for the chess club, he would have known on which evenings Wallace was playing chess matches. Why did Parry conceal these assignations from Wallace? But far, more importantly, why did Julia? If they were innocent there was no reason to do so. Goodman himself writes in *The Killing of Julia Wallace*:

> … the robbery motive must not be ruled out and neither must the sex motive. Just because Julia was middle-aged, unattractive to most men, does not nec-essarily mean that she was undesirable to a man who's Oedipus complex had gone completely haywire in a mess of distorted sexual urges. The very fact that she was middle aged and unattractive might have made her irresistibly

desirable. Perhaps Parry and Julia, with Wallace safely out of the way were, making their own kind of music .

Goodman interprets these facts in support of the idea that Parry was the murderer. But surely this can lead to a very different conclusion. Parry's refusal, when interviewed, to speak of the Wallace case, may have been due to the fact that although he himself was not the murderer, he knew full well that his own actions had brought the crime about. Did Wallace discover the affair, and if so when? This question is a matter of conjecture. What is certain is that if he had found out the truth the effect on Wallace would have been catastrophic. To Wallace the revelation that the icon of his life was being unfaithful would have been totally devastating. The dangerous consequences which can result from the insertion of a young and unprincipled man into a marriage is too clearly shown by the Thompson–Bywaters case.

The reaction of a cuckolded husband varies greatly, according to the circumstances and the character of the parties involved; but Wallace, had he decided upon murder, in keeping with his nature, would have planned the act coolly and methodically, in keeping with his stoical philosophy. 'If I cannot have her nobody else will' is not an unknown emotion behind many a homicide.

By all reports, Julia Wallace was a mild, well-behaved, church-going lady. An admirable person by all accounts. That is why I couch the above words merely as a question – not an accusation, but no human being is totally exempt from temptation – including the temptation of illicit passion. The degree of planning behind Julia's murder is not inconsistent with what Professor MacFall describes as 'A frenzied attack'. And, for all the criticism made of his use of this expression, MacFall was a highly experienced forensic expert. Was it the murder of Julia Wallace by Qualtrough that shattered Wallace's life to smithereens, or was it the discovery of her infidelity of which her murder was the consequence. We shall never know for sure.

POSTSCRIPT

Why do people murder their spouses or lovers? Are these types of murder different in kind from others? And if so, should they be punished differently? And why?

In England we do not have the Scottish verdict of 'not proven'. It seems unfair to the accused. The defendant is set free, but carries the stigma that he has not been declared innocent, merely that the case cannot, and has not been, proved against him or her. Nor in Britain is there the French doctrine of *crime passionel*. Capital punishment has been abolished but murder remains murder. The prosecution may accept a plea of guilty to the lesser charge of manslaughter, but that is within the discretion of the Crown. The judge cannot direct them to do so. Once murder has been established the relatively new provision of diminished responsibility may apply.

Section 2 of the Homicide Act of 1957 provides:

1   Where a person kills or is party to the killing of another, he shall not be convicted of murder if he was suffering from such abnormality of mind (whether arising from a condition of arrested or retarded development of mind or any inherent causes or induced by disease or injury) as subsequently impaired his mental responsibility for his acts and omissions in doing or being a party to the killing.

With regard to manslaughter, in the case of *Saunders* (1988), the defendant was charged with murder. The jury eventually made it clear that, although they were agreed upon manslaughter, a majority of them could not agree upon murder. They were permitted to return a verdict of manslaughter and were discharged from returning a verdict of murder.

There are two forms of manslaughter, voluntary and involuntary. Voluntary manslaughter occurs when all the elements of murder are present, including an intent to kill or cause grievous bodily harm, but the crime is reduced to manslaughter by reason of:

(a)   provocation;

(b)   diminished responsibility;

(c)   death being caused in pursuance of a suicide pact.

Involuntary manslaughter is unlawful killing without intent to kill or cause grievous bodily harm, see *Taylor* (1834).

It is proposed in this final section to examine, by way of comparison with the Wallace case, some of the notable murder trials of the 19th and 20th centuries. It is surprising that many of them involve defendants, who, like Wallace, cannot be adjudged psychopathic killers, although these are a familiar type in criminal history. They are apparently normal people who have over reacted through rage or a sense of personal injustice, or who have become trapped in a situation which drives them to a desperate remedy for their problems. This is not, of course to minimise the heinousness of their crimes.

Madeleine Smith was a young Scottish girl of good family who fell in love with a French packing-clerk named L'Angelier. Madeleine, during their somewhat clandestine courtship, had written a number of love letters to the young Frenchman. When she, in due course, became engaged to a more 'appropriate' suitor she was very anxious to recover the passionate letters. L'Angelier began to suffer from severe stomach pains, and in due course died in great agony. An autopsy disclosed the presence of a very large quantity of arsenic in his stomach. Madeleine protested that she had not seen L'Angelier recently and knew nothing of his ailment. However it was discovered that she had made purchases of arsenic, which she maintained was used externally to improve her complexion. Madeleine Smith was charged in 1857 with the murder of her erstwhile lover, but the jury returned a verdict of 'not proven'.

In 1885, Adelaide Bartlett was charged with the murder of her husband by administering to him a quantity of chloroform which was subsequently found to be present in his stomach. A young Methodist minister named the Reverend George Dyson was charged with being an accessory. As a young girl of 19, Adelaide had become trapped in a loveless marriage with a husband a great deal older than herself. Mr Bartlett even sent his young wife to boarding school, and on her return paid her scant attention. He rejected her wish to have children and her life became lonely and friendless. The entry of a cultured young man onto the scene was a classic ingredient for trouble. Dyson, the newly-found friend of Adelaide purchased a quantity of chloroform allegedly to 'calm' her husband; but at his death both were charged with his murder. In the event both were acquitted.

In 1889, Florence Maybrick was charged with the murder of her husband James Maybrick by poisoning him with arsenic. The marriage contained the classic scenario for a disturbed relationship. Florence at the time of the marriage was 18; her husband was 41. Two children were born of their marriage, but within nine years of matrimony things started to go badly wrong. Mrs Maybrick took a lover, and Mr Maybrick on occasions became physically violent towards his wife. When Maybrick took to his bed with symptoms of illness caused by stomach pains she purchased fly papers impregnated with arsenic. This she was charged with administering to him, having soaked the fly papers in water to extract the arsenic. The amount was far less than in the case of Adelaide Bartlett, but the jury found her guilty of murder. After her release from imprisonment she continued to protest her innocence.

The case of Edith Thompson in 1923 was another sad example of what can happen when an emotionally wayward young woman is married to an older man and a younger and attractive figure intervenes. Edith wrote letters to Frederick Bywaters, by whom she had become besotted, which appeared to encourage Byewaters to murder her husband. When the latter stabbed Mr Thompson however, Edith was heard to shout 'oh don't, oh don't'. Notwithstanding her change of heart the jury convicted Edith for what some would say was a judgement on her morals rather than her position in law and both she and her lover were executed.

For many people marriage provides a sound basis for a happy and fulfilling life. For some it proves to be a failed relationship, and for a few, as we have seen, it precipitates disaster.

In 1905 Arthur Devereux was charged with the murder of his wife and twin sons. Devereux was a chemist's assistant who poisoned the victims with the contents of a bottle of morphine, which he had brought home from his shop. His defence, that his wife had committed suicide and then killed the children, was firmly rejected by the jury and Devereux was executed, still protesting his innocence. Devereux had severe financial problems supporting his wife and family on a small income. He chose murder as a way of escape from his difficulties. The callous manner in which he stuffed the bodies into a trunk, which he left in a warehouse, won him little sympathy.

It is sometimes said that the alternative option of divorce was not, in practice, available to ordinary people in that period. Yet husband and wife homicide continues today when matrimonial breakdown is more easily catered for by the law.

In the case of Dr Hawley Harvey Crippen in 1910 it was a young woman rather than a young man who caused Crippen to seek the ultimate way out of a marriage which had proved a disaster. The married couple moved to London in 1898, there the relationship deteriorated. Crippen earned little as the manager of a patent medicine company, and Cora his wife tried to make a name for herself as a music hall star. Her talent, however, extended to acquiring lovers and spending money on what she thought would further

her ambitions, but to little more. Into this collapsing partnership came Ethel Le Neve, an attractive young typist. She and Crippen became lovers. This only accentuated the animosity between Crippen and Cora with the latter threatening to leave and to draw money out of their joint bank account. Cora disappeared and Crippen gave various reasons for her absence. A friend of Cora contacted the police and Crippen and Ethel took ship to America. They were arrested, brought back to England and tried. Crippen was convicted and hanged, Ethel was acquitted. The dismembered remains of Cora had been discovered in the coal cellar of the house where she and he husband had lived. Why didn't the pair simply elope? This would surely have been the simplest solution, and there would have been little that Cora could have done about it.

Some wife and husband killers have been consummately evil people, such as George Smith of the 'brides in the bath' cases. Others have been simply greedy for the money which might be forthcoming as the result of their spouse's death. Others are weak people who have been overwhelmed by events which drove them to a desperate remedy.

Which of these was Wallace? Or could he have been innocent? I leave my readers to decide.

INDEX